Praise

'This book is a brilliant and beautiful p.—
It is a thoroughly enjoyable read that includes a lot
of substance and great anecdotes from Natasa and
Jim's personal experiences as airline executives. I am
convinced that anyone with even a hint of interest in
improving his or her health, fitness, wellbeing and
life generally will benefit from this book, because its
insights and suggestions are real-life, tangible and
achievable for the reader.'
  — **Henning zur Hausen**, General Counsel,
    Etihad Aviation Group

'Amongst all the noise about what's healthy and
what's not, *Ready for TAKEOFF!* stands out with a
holistic view and a simple and practical application.
The four drivers of health make so much sense,
but it is the TAKEOFF model that really makes
those principles easy to apply, even if you are
extremely busy and constantly on the road. If you
like straightforward, scientifically backed yet easy
to read, practical books, you will love this one.'
  — **Melinda Kecskes**, co-founder of Wizz Air,
    aviation and travel brand expert

'*Ready for TAKEOFF!* unlocks the secrets to healthy
habits that can help sustain the energy required to
meet the demands of working in the fast-paced and
crisis-prone industry that is aviation. Natasa and
Jim have studied the science, tested the practices,

and created a comprehensive, easy-to-apply roadmap combining four key elements: mindset, healthy eating, moving more and sleeping better. It is a great investment in your health, so buckle up and get ready for TAKEOFF!'

— **Emese Bekessy**, former senior airline executive

'Many people take their health for granted as they move higher up the corporate ladder. But the unhealthy habits we fall into eventually lead to rapid ageing and leave us prone to a higher risk of disease and burnout. In *Ready for TAKEOFF!* Natasa and Jim share their powerful stories and provide a message of hope: that we can maintain our health and perform at a much higher level by following some simple but powerful principles. I'm applying these principles in my own life and have personally witnessed the benefits for my health and performance.'

— **Marco Nindl**, senior banker

'Living the life and living the dream are often two different things, but with this industry-specific playbook for creating balance, Kazmer and Callaghan outline the pragmatic building blocks required to do both. The book distils their lived experience in the aviation industry and details the results of their commitment to researching solutions, creating an approachable starting place from which to regain and enhance wellbeing. From its opening chapter highlighting the importance of mindset, the book takes a holistic and achievable view of the factors that go into supporting a healthy lifestyle, while managing and progressing a demanding career in aviation.'

— **Deirdre Morrison**, co-founder, NeuroDevelopment Institute

READY FOR TAKEOFF!

A practical health guide for airline executives and their teams to get back on top of their game

NATASA KAZMER AND JIM CALLAGHAN

Rethink

First published in Great Britain in 2023 by Rethink Press
(www.rethinkpress.com)

This book is dedicated to all our colleagues in the airline industry who work tirelessly to keep the world connected.

Contents

Foreword

Dear reader,

Your body is your business. Nobody else will take care of it for you. What you do to or for your body impacts every aspect of your life.

Would you board an aircraft that operates twenty-four hours a day, seven days a week, that hasn't been maintained for years and uses fuel that has been contaminated with impurities? 'Of course not!' I hear you say. Yet have you ever wondered why we meticulously maintain and fuel our aircraft for safe, optimal performance, while we neglect the very machines that transport us throughout our lives – our bodies and minds?

As the founder and chief excellence officer of FiiT4GROWTH, an executive coaching and training company that specialises in high-performance coaching for commercial leaders and their teams, I understand the importance of maintaining a healthy lifestyle to achieve excellence and growth. I've had the privilege of working with executives and their teams in thirty-three countries around the world, in various sectors, from top global brands in fast-moving consumer goods to hospitality, healthcare, education, retail and civil service. What I consistently found during this experience, regardless of the industry or country I was working in, was that corporate cultures celebrated achievement at all costs, while their people were burning out.

The High Performance Institute states that the key to high performance, far from encouraging this 'at all costs' attitude, is 'achieving above standard norms, consistently over the long term, while maintaining wellbeing and positive relationships'.[1] That's why I'm excited to introduce you to *Ready for TAKEOFF!*, a comprehensive guidebook that provides practical advice, inspiring stories and actionable tips to achieve optimal health and peak performance.

This book aims to answer the central question of how executives, particularly those in the aviation industry, can maintain optimal health and peak performance while balancing the demands of a fast-paced, high-stress career. The authors, Natasa and Jim, both experienced the ill-effects of neglecting their health while pursuing their careers in the airline industry, and they recognised the need for a complete change of mindset and an uncompromising commitment to health.

I've known Natasa and Jim since early 2022, when we met in a community of wellness entrepreneurs looking to make a dent in the universe. From the very first interaction, I could see their passion and commitment to helping people realise that there is a better approach to work and life. They turned their pain into purpose, and have built a business around their expertise, enabling them to share their knowledge, strategies and practical tactics.

Both Natasa and Jim have achieved incredible personal wellness results. They are equipped with empathy for those struggling with challenges like those they faced with their mental and physical health, and they've created a model to help others overcome similar obstacles. They have also invested significant time and energy in researching the science and best strategies to achieve optimal health. I've experienced their vibrancy and enthusiasm, and have seen them consistently implement the strategies they teach in their own lives. They are wonderful human beings, with hearts to serve, and a strong desire to create positive change and make a significant impact in the world.

This book is ideal for *anyone* looking to take their personal or professional life to the next level. Whether you're in the aviation industry, an entrepreneur launching a new business, a student embarking on a new career or simply someone looking to make a positive change in your life, this book is an invaluable resource.

The book is divided into three parts. Part One, 'Our Story', recounts the personal wellness journeys of the authors, which serve as a reminder that true health is not about a quick fix but is a lifelong commitment. In Part Two, 'The Four Drivers of Health', each chapter covers one of the key drivers of health: mindset, nutrition, movement and sleep. The authors provide practical advice and insights into how modern lifestyles have affected our health, explaining the importance of each driver and how they are interconnected.

Finally, Part Three sets out Natasa and Jim's TAKEOFF model, a framework that enables people to reclaim their health and supercharge their performance. The principles in each area are based on science and designed to ensure the biggest impact for health and performance.

Overall, *Ready for TAKEOFF!* is an outstanding book that I highly recommend to anyone looking to unlock their full potential. Congratulations to Natasa and Jim for creating such a powerful and valuable resource, and to you, the reader, for embarking on this journey to new levels of personal and professional performance. Apply the principles in this book, and you will be amazed at the transformation. Buckle up and enjoy the ride!

John Roussot
Multi-award-winning business coach and leadership
　　development trainer
Founder and Chief Excellence Officer, FiiT4GROWTH
Author of *Liberate Your Greatness*
johnroussot.com ｜ fiit4growth.com

Introduction

As aviation folks, we appreciate the miracle of flight – the ability of a multi-tonne machine to defy gravity and soar above the clouds. The sheer complexity and number of parts and components in a modern aircraft are mind-boggling. We also understand that meticulous maintenance and proper fuelling of an aircraft are critical for ensuring safe and efficient operations.

And yet, when it comes to our own bodies, we seem to take them completely for granted. Often, we use this machine, which is far more complex and adaptable than any aircraft, simply to transport us throughout our lives, without care or concern for the amazing abilities of our bodies and minds, or the need for their ongoing attention and maintenance.

Inevitably, as a result, our health and performance levels start to deteriorate. We can get away with putting our bodies through a lot of abuse when we're young, but as we mature and progress through our challenging careers in aviation – one of the most intense and competitive industries in the world – our lack of focus on health and wellbeing begins to take a serious toll, on both a physical and a mental level.

This is where we, Jim and Natasa, found ourselves at the height of our own careers in some of the best-known airlines in the world. Jim started his aviation career as General Counsel and Company Secretary for Ryanair, Europe's leading low-cost airline and one of the most famous (some would say 'infamous') airlines in the world. After nine years in the wars with Ryanair, he moved to Etihad Airways, a premium Middle Eastern carrier and one facing many of the same competitive pressures as Ryanair, but in a different segment of the market.

Natasa is a co-founder of Wizz Air, one of the largest low-cost airlines in Europe and recognised throughout the world. She started her career in the Hungarian national airline, Malév, where her father also worked as an engineer, so she truly has aviation in her blood! She was Head of Corporate Communications and Public Affairs at Wizz Air, and at the peak of her career she also set up and managed Wizz Air Ukraine, a highly successful subsidiary of Wizz Air.

We both put our hearts and souls into the business, almost above all else, but over time, we each started to experience the ill effects of our fast-paced, career-focused lives. Tasks that were run-of-the-mill at an earlier stage in our careers started to become more challenging. We noticed a drop in energy, lack of motivation and decreased focus. We started to get sick more often, and small niggling things started to turn into more concerning symptoms over time. We also began to doubt the sustainability of this lifestyle and our ability to continue to perform at our highest levels, both at work and at home.

People working in the airline industry are, by and large, extremely passionate about what they do. Connecting people and delivering all nature of products around the globe is inspirational. However, it is also one of the most challenging and stressful industries in the world, with some form of crisis or other continuously arising. This constant pressure and stress starts to take its toll on employees. They often start to experience nagging health issues, low energy and sometimes even anxiety and depression. They may self-medicate through alcohol, caffeine, junk food and other vices. If unaddressed, these problems quickly lead to more serious health issues, which can profoundly impact one's career and quality of life generally.

This book is the result of our own journeys to rediscover our health and reach a realisation that health is incredibly precious and shouldn't be taken for granted. Equally important, is that by being healthy we can be more focused and productive, both at work and in our personal lives. Put differently, we don't have to sacrifice our health for career success – health actually drives greater levels of success. The results of our experiences made us want to share our stories and our unique model for achieving peak health and performance with colleagues who are struggling with their own health and performance.

Part One of the book sets out our own individual wellness stories. We both started out with very different backgrounds, and we each had our own health challenges. Although we realised at various points that we needed to tackle these issues, often taking drastic measures to address the symptoms, these efforts were usually short-lived and didn't address the true causes of the problem. Luckily, we had the opportunity during Covid to refocus on our individual health issues. What started to emerge for both of us was that true health is not about a quick-fix, knee-jerk reaction to a perceived problem. It involves a complete change of mindset and an uncompromising, lifelong commitment to your health.

We also discovered that the secret to sustainable peak performance is … well, health. More and more scientists, researchers, health coaches and doctors agree that optimal health is built on four key drivers: mindset, nutrition, movement and sleep. And they all require an equal level of focus. It's not enough to have a positive mindset but let your nutrition, movement and sleep go to hell. Similarly, you can have the healthiest of diets but lead a sedentary lifestyle and, as a result, be unhealthy.

This realisation led us to establish Wellnesstory, our health coaching company, which is dedicated to the concept that no one should have to sacrifice their health for career success. We also know the challenges that everyone faces in terms of time constraints and stress levels, so we've taken the stress out of being healthy by making it as convenient and straightforward as possible. Understanding the key principles behind health drives a strong mindset and motivation to adopt the healthy habits that form the building blocks to a healthy mind and body. Making small, incremental and consistent changes makes the process effective, efficient and sustainable.

Part Two discusses the four drivers of health. Each chapter covers one of the drivers and starts by explaining how we evolved in each area and how these evolutionary adaptations served us well for millennia, helping us to operate at peak capacity. Unfortunately, in many cases, our modern lifestyles are actually working against this evolutionary 'programming'. The natural rhythms we evolved around have been replaced by an overabundant, always-on culture, which is wreaking havoc on our health.

Although we're not professional doctors, psychologists or dietitians, we have taken the time to dive deep into the science behind each area. We were shocked to find the extent to which modern lifestyle is responsible for the current epidemic in the so-called 'lifestyle diseases', including obesity, heart disease, diabetes, cancer and dementia.

Finally, Part Three sets out our TAKEOFF model, which is a framework that enables you to reclaim your health and supercharge your performance by working *with* your evolutionary programming. The principles of the model are based on the most up-to-date science in each area, and we've put them in a format that ensures the biggest bang for your buck. In other words, we don't waste your time on things that won't significantly move the needle on your health and performance. Nevertheless, if you are interested in learning more, we've included references and a Suggested Further Reading section. You can also check out our website www.wellnesstory.world for additional resources.

This is not a 'quick fix' solution. Our declining health is a product of years of ignorance and neglect, and it won't be fixed in a day. It will take time. The good news is that with the right mindset and motivation, and by following the principles set out in this book, you can achieve optimal health and peak performance and maintain it for the rest of your life. It might also significantly increase your health span, ie the number of years that you experience a healthy life (as opposed to living with serious disease and constant aches and pains).

Our wellness stories are never-ending. We keep amending, updating and improving them at each stage of our lives to ensure that we remain in peak health and can perform at our highest levels. The TAKEOFF model is designed to be applicable at any point in your life and at any level of fitness. It's an iterative process starting out with small, consistent steps that help to build healthy habits, each layering on top of the other. Following and repeating the model will keep delivering levels of health and performance you probably never realised were possible.

So, are you ready for TAKEOFF?

PART ONE
OUR STORY

Stories are powerful. From early on in our evolution, and long before the written word, we humans learned to tell stories. This helped us share knowledge and create bonds within our families, tribes and, eventually, wider communities. Stories appeal to our emotions. We love a good book or movie that takes us on a rollercoaster of emotions but leaves us feeling good in the end. Our brains have therefore evolved to receive and process information more efficiently through stories. We also feel an emotional connection with the storyteller – we can see ourselves in them, feel their emotions and identify with their struggles.

As well as listening to stories, we tell stories, and the most important stories are the ones we tell ourselves. Our whole life is a story, and we convince ourselves that we *are* our story. It feels 'real'. Through our memories, we can even play recordings of our story in our head over and over again. But we are not our stories, and we can change our storyline at any time. As Michael Margolis, founder and CEO of Storied, says: 'The stories we tell literally make the world. If you want to change the world, you need to change your story.'[2]

This is why we spend time sharing our individual stories in this book. Many of you will be able to identify with our struggles of trying to juggle health with busy careers and relationships, in an increasingly stressful and disconnected world. Stress and concern over declining health are also probably among the most discussed topics on social media these days. There is information overload out there, and it can become overwhelming. Whose story do we listen to? What recent scientific breakthrough is applicable to us?

Hopefully, our stories of struggling with but ultimately rediscovering our health will resonate with you and give you hope that it *is* possible to find that balance between health and success in our careers and life generally. In fact, success can only truly be experienced if we are physically and mentally healthy.

So, pull up a comfy chair, pour yourself a hot drink and read about our wellness journeys. Hopefully they will inspire you to rewrite your own story.

1
Natasa And Jim

Natasa

I grew up in the Soviet Union and Hungary in the 1980s, when supermarkets were pretty much empty and cars were a luxury. We sourced most of our food from the farmers' market, where the produce was fresh and seasonal. That meant no year-round strawberries, but it taught me to appreciate vegetables and fruits when they were in season. My grandparents grew most of their own food, made tons of preserves and stored potatoes, carrots and apples for winter. As far as exercise was concerned, as there was a relative absence of cars, we walked a lot and used public transport. Although my parents focused more on my academic development, they also made sure I had plenty of physical activity. I started swimming at the age of four and spent a lot of time outdoors skipping and playing a variety of team sports.

When I was a bit older, we spent most of my summer holidays travelling in the Soviet Union to places like Lake Baykal in the east, Uzbekistan, Azerbaijan, Armenia and Georgia in the south, and Ukraine in the west. We visited my extended family, friends and friends of friends. Looking back, what stands out for me is how much of these visits were spent around the table. The food was incredible. It was always local, fresh and seasonal. But most importantly, we spent this time with people that we loved. These were truly joyful and happy times. I learned that food, in all cultures, is used to express love and caring. This remains a guiding principle in my life. Eating together is so much more than ensuring the appropriate caloric intake. It is a physical and emotional replenishment. We should remember this, especially when yet another diet fails us.

My happy young adulthood days ended when my dad passed away from colon cancer after a gruesome six-year battle. He was only forty-four. After his death, I started to have panic attacks. The psychiatrist explained to me that it was the result of the chronic stress my brain had experienced during the years of my father's illness.

In an interesting twist of fate, after my studies, I ended up working for Malév. I stepped into my dad's shoes, in a way. It was the late 1990s and the winds of change were blowing strongly in the airline industry. A smart and ambitious manager was appointed to the helm of the airline a few months prior to 9/11. I joined his team as a business assistant, and later, as a project manager. The terrorist attacks on 9/11 sped up reforms within Malév, and before I knew it, I was running large, complex projects such as the overhaul of the airline's frequent flyer programme with McKinsey, and the Malév-KLM alliance. But, as we all know in the airline industry, governments do not have good track records of owning airlines, and eventually politics forced the CEO and his team (including me) out.

I believe that things happen for a reason. About a year after the team and I left, we launched Wizz Air, together with five ex-colleagues from Malév. At the time of writing, Wizz Air is one of the most successful airlines in Europe. I was thirty-one, ambitious and hungry for success. We grew at lightning speed and were soon competing with giants like Ryanair. I was Head of Corporate Communications and Public Affairs, always on the road to meet regulatory bodies, speak with journalists, launch new flights and discuss big ideas at conferences. In 2008, I set up and managed Wizz Air Ukraine. It was the most stressful, and the most rewarding, experience of my career. I was working around the clock but loved every single moment of it.

I lived and breathed success. I was an adrenaline and dopamine junky without realising it. My body and mind were operating at 110% most of the time, but I was handling it – or so I thought. There was nothing that could have predicted what would happen next.

In 2009, my life was turned upside down when I fell in love with Jim. It was a tsunami that whisked me out of my well-established role of co-founder and communications expert and, only a year later, took me to Abu Dhabi to become a partner and 'housewife'. That's when my body decided it was payback time. To my surprise, I fell into a depression. I was with the love of my life, in a beautiful place and surrounded by luxury, and yet I felt like I was falling apart. My hormones gave up first. My monthly cycle stopped, and I was diagnosed with insulin resistance. I turned to the one thing I knew to be the key to happiness – food. We were eating out most of the time and my extra five kilos became a permanent layer of fat on my body.

Eventually, I had to take a step back to redefine my sense of identity without my role at Wizz Air, which I felt was an integral part of who I was. In doing so, I found a mindfulness practice that worked for me and went back to study the connection between human happiness and corporate success. This was something that I was truly passionate about and it helped me not only to grow professionally, but also personally. All this hard work on myself also led to a breakthrough in my relationship with Jim and he proposed. We were married in 2014.

But just like being on a rollercoaster, the next few years were a struggle again – this time, with my fertility. At the age of forty-one, I was not the youngest prospective mother, but I did not expect it to be so difficult. At the time, my doctor pointed out that my whole body, including my egg cells, were chronically stressed. I couldn't understand how this could be the case. I was not working, and we had a cleaner, a gardener and a pool attendant. I did nothing that even vaguely resembled a stressful activity. But I also hadn't done enough, physically or emotionally, to heal my body after years of corporate stress. Now it had come back to haunt me. It took me five cycles of IVF treatment to become pregnant. In 2017, at almost forty-four, I gave birth to an amazing baby boy, just a few months after we moved to Amsterdam. Unfortunately, my struggles did not end there.

After the birth, I had full-blown postpartum depression and, to top it off, I was seriously sleep deprived. I was also mostly eating sandwiches that were easy to make with a baby in my arms. After I stopped breastfeeding, I was still around 20 kilos overweight. Eventually, I started working out with a personal trainer and engaged a nutritionist. Neither helped. My weight was not moving, I hated my meal plan and I struggled with my workouts. Eventually, I fell off the wagon completely. I was constantly tired and still overweight. I kept feeling that I was missing a critical piece of the puzzle.

In 2019, we moved to Haarlem, a beautiful city around 20 minutes from Amsterdam. Finally, I felt settled and something also clicked in terms of my overall mindset. It was then that Jim and I finally decided to commit to whatever it took to get our health in order. I wanted to feel good in my body again, be a better spouse for Jim and a vibrant and patient mother for our son, Daniel.

Jim

Turning fifty was an interesting milestone for me. I didn't feel 'old', but I was definitely tired. Truth be told, I had been feeling exhausted for a long time, probably since my late thirties. I went to several doctors to try to find out what was 'wrong' with me, but generally came back with a clean bill of health. A bit overweight, but nothing too critical. So, why did it feel like I was only living a 'half-life' – too exhausted to fully engage and feeling as though I was always underperforming?

It hadn't always been that way. As a child, I was fortunate to grow up on a small farm in Ireland. We grew a lot of our own food and had access to locally sourced meat. In terms of physical activity, working on a farm is perhaps the closest thing you can get to primal living. Lots of lifting, climbing, carrying, squatting, etc. I also played sports, when I wasn't shovelling cow shit! Talk about a healthy upbringing.

When I finished secondary school, I moved from Ireland to the US for college and law school. That's when my health started to go off the rails. I fully embraced the Standard American Diet ('SAD' – very sad). Fast food was my staple. I could eat six tacos from Taco Bell, along with a litre of Pepsi and a serving of Churros for dessert. This, all while sitting on the couch watching movies (on the VCR, in the days before Netflix). A recipe for eventual disaster.

Of course, pursuing the American dream meant working full-time while studying, so I spent a lot of time sitting at a desk, either at university or the law firm where I worked as a clerk. I was doing very little exercise in those days, with the exception of walking to and from the train station. This trend continued throughout my twenties and early thirties during law school and my first years in private practice. In addition, I had a massive amount of work stress. After completing a masters in law in Brussels, I started my first 'real' job at a top law firm. By then, my first wife and I had two beautiful sons. I was working on huge commercial transactions – the Exxon-Mobil merger was the largest ever at that time. But there was little time for anything else, including my health and family life.

Fast forward ten years. I was the father of four wonderful boys and 'living the dream', career-wise. We had moved to Ireland and I spent nine years in the war zone at Ryanair headquarters in Dublin as Director of Legal and Regulatory Affairs and also as Company

Secretary. This was during a time when the airline grew tenfold in terms of passenger numbers. I spent a lot of time in courts all over Europe defending the low-fares model. The constant travelling, and all the bad eating habits and lack of exercise that go along with it, took its toll. My sleep pattern was also disrupted (too many 6am flights to Brussels to lobby the European Commission). My sons used to complain that I was always on the phone at weekends and while we were on holidays, which was true, and I understood their frustration. The sense of being a 'bad parent' is a pretty potent stressor.

By the time I moved to Abu Dhabi to head up Etihad Airway's legal team, my health and relationships were crumbling. At home, my marriage was suffering, as was my relationship with my kids. I was constantly stressed out and bad tempered. I found it difficult to separate my work and home life, and my mental and physical health were suffering. I tried various diets and workout regimes, some of which had a positive impact for a period of time, but I always reverted back to unhealthy habits when things became busy at work or stressful at home.

I eventually got divorced and suffered a lot of guilt over it, as well as having separation anxiety from my kids. Stress at work was even worse and changing jobs hadn't helped. Unfortunately, we tend to make the same mistakes until we finally tackle the root of the problem.

I had known Natasa for several years through various industry events and our involvement in a low-fares airline association I helped to establish while I was at Ryanair. There was no romantic involvement at the time – she used to say that she liked me for my brain more than anything else! But, at a subconscious level, I think we could identify with each other's career struggles. Around the time I was moving to Etihad, we started to become closer and she eventually moved out to the Middle East while I was at Etihad. That was a challenging time for both of us, but also a joyful time.

By the time we had our son, Daniel, I was forty-eight and had changed jobs again, this time moving to Amsterdam to join Uber as General Counsel for Europe, Middle East and Africa. I saw Uber as a kind of 'Ryanair without the wings' because of all of its regulatory challenges. I seem to go from one frying pan to a larger fire each time I move jobs. Ultimately, it led to burnout for me. After working for several months at Uber, under severe stress, I experienced strange breakdowns during a number of key meetings. My speech became slurred and I struggled to make any sense. It was frightening, to say the least. I was also having heart palpitations at night, which were disrupting my sleep. At that stage I knew I had to make some radical changes.

I took some time off from work to be with Natasa and Daniel and started my own aviation consulting business (I'd had enough of ground transportation). I slowly started to be more conscious about what I was eating and began moving more. But, as with previous experiences, being busy setting up the new consultancy and not really knowing how to attack my health problems properly meant that I was flailing around in the dark and not making significant progress.

It wasn't until my fiftieth birthday that I made a concerted commitment to systematically improve my health to be a better version of myself for Natasa and a better father for my five boys. With Natasa at a similar level of frustration, and also committed to change, we started our own wellness journeys. These would eventually culminate in us founding our health coaching business, Wellnesstory.

2
Our Wellnesstory

In 2019, we moved from Amsterdam to Haarlem. After years of struggling with our individual health issues, we could no longer continue on the path of just 'trying things', because we were not getting any better. On the contrary, we were becoming tired, middle-aged people with constant low energy, poor moods and aches and pains. But how could we possibly commit to any path when there was so much information out there that was often confusing and contradictory? Is coffee good or bad? Should we go keto or paleo? Is red wine good for your heart? Should we join the 5am club, start meditating, running 10k? The list goes on and on.

Which of the latest trends was 'right' for us? To make things even more difficult, most of the advice involved making a massive change to our lifestyle and a huge time commitment. We were also trying to figure out how to adopt a healthy lifestyle as busy people and as a *family*. What is it that would work for our different genders, ages, life stages and, most importantly, our busy lives. Jim was still heavily involved with his consulting business and Natasa was travelling a lot for her leadership coaching. We also had the small matter of a three-year-old to raise and Jim travelling to Ireland often to spend time with his other boys. We were overwhelmed and frustrated, but we knew we needed a change that would result in a sustainable, healthy lifestyle for us.

We recognised that whenever we 'fell off the wagon', we had a very hard time getting back on track. A small slice of chocolate cake was able to ruin two weeks of good efforts. We simply did not have a good enough reason to keep improving our health. Losing ten kilos to look good for a class reunion or upcoming wedding was all too superficial. We had to find a reason so important, so personal and so meaningful that it would keep us going even when it became challenging. In the words of Simon Sinek in his book *Start with Why: How Great Leaders Inspire Everyone to Take Action*, we had to find our deepest 'Why'.[3]

Luckily, our corporate backgrounds and Natasa's positive leadership and strategy studies proved useful. At one point, we literally had a formal strategy meeting and used a positive psychology framework called Appreciative Inquiry (AI)[4] to help co-create our healthy future. Developed in the early 1990s by David Cooperrider and Suresh Srivastva, we found the process invaluable. It made us focus on the big picture and find our true motivation, our 'Why', to create positive change. It started by answering these questions:

- Where do we want to be/how do we want to *feel* in five to ten years and beyond?

- What are the key things we want to achieve?

- What do we enjoy doing the most?

- What is our belief system around our health?

- What would become possible for us if we get this right?

Our answers completely changed the way we thought of health. We realised that it was not something *on top* of everything we had to do, but that health was, indeed, the *enabler* of the life we really wanted to live. We knew from experience that our bodies and minds were resistant to change and would do anything to sabotage us. It's called 'cognitive bias', a psychological mechanism that makes it difficult to accept or implement change.[5] By being aware of this bias, we could now override this resistance to start making the necessary changes. We were committed because our reasons were meaningful and powerful to us. We were confident because we had the right mindset.

We knew we would succeed, because we knew what success actually meant.

With that commitment in place, we made our first conscious step and chose a physical activity that was right for *us*. We joined the local CrossFit box. The reason we chose CrossFit over any of the numerous gyms in and around Haarlem was because the philosophy of this particular sport resonated with us. It focuses on full body, functional movements and has a strong community element. We loved the workouts and also enjoyed the chats with other CrossFitters after the classes.

In February 2020, just as Covid started to wreak serious havoc in our lives and all around the world, Natasa became seriously ill after a trip to London. Searching for natural ways to recover more quickly, she found a nutritional programme called WILDFIT. It claimed to reset gut health and restore the gut-brain connection, thus supporting overall health. It combined behavioural science, human evolution and nutrition. Jim also followed the programme (in the beginning, mostly out of support for Natasa). The changes in our physical bodies, energy levels and mood were mind-blowing. And as an additional benefit, the CrossFit workouts also started to bring real results in terms of strength and endurance. We were on fire!

We became increasingly curious and hungry to learn more, so we both began to delve deeper into nutrition and fitness. Natasa did a programme with Stanford on Nutrition Science and Jim completed a Stanford course on the Physiology of Exercise. Other programmes followed, including more nutrition qualifications for Natasa and Jim completing the Level 1 Training Certificate for coaching CrossFit.

We were learning and applying the principles relating to nutrition and movement in our own lives, but even with all that wealth of information, some changes were incredibly hard. We started to connect the dots and became conscious of the fact that how we think and talk about ourselves influences our physical and mental health. We began to recognise how powerful habits were and how difficult it was to break old, unhealthy ones to introduce new, healthier ones.

As a last frontier, we also started to pay more attention to our sleep. This is, by far, the most neglected driver of health. Good quality sleep is not only fundamental to our wellbeing, it also significantly impacts the efficiency of the other drivers of our health. We established a pretty solid sleep routine, and while we are by no means fanatical about it (we still occasionally stay up to watch a good show on Netflix), we are consistent 90% of the time and we have seen significant results.

This formed the basis for our four drivers of health approach to our wellness journey: having a health-centric mindset, eating well, moving function-ally and getting good sleep. Optimal health requires taking action in each of these areas. Jim likes to say that health is like a table. If you lose one leg, it becomes unstable. If you lose more than one leg, it falls over.

In terms of our own physical results during this pro-cess, Natasa lost about 10 kilos, but this only tells part of the story as she also gained a significant amount of lean muscle mass (and muscles are heavier than fat). So, her overall body composition was far more impressive than what the scales were saying. Simi-larly, Jim lost around 12 kilos (most of which was fat), and has subsequently replaced some of that weight with additional lean muscle mass. From an athletic point of view, both of us were shocked by the mas-sive improvement in the performance of our bodies. We had both been involved in sports to some degree when we were young, but at this stage in our lives, we did not imagine being able to perform complex gymnastics movements, to engage in high-intensity exercises or to lift as much weight from a strength point of view as we now could.

Although we both hate 'before and after' photos, pictures often speak for themselves. The left photo below is Natasa about eight months after our son Daniel's birth. The one on the right is two years after we embarked on our wellness journeys. Quite a transformation.

The left photo below is Jim holding Daniel on the same holiday as Natasa above. (No, he is not pregnant!) The one on the right is him competing in a CrossFit competition after only two years of following the principles we had developed based on the four health drivers.

Perhaps even more important than our physical transformations are the remarkable changes to our energy levels and productivity, not to mention a significant improvement in our moods. Jim had struggled with energy levels since his law school days, but started to find his energy and focus were higher than at any point over the past twenty-five years. Natasa also found her energy levels much improved, and she stopped being the 'moody mama bear' she used to be. The afternoon energy dips, the headaches and the constant cravings were gone, too. She was also getting through a lot more work in a day than she had been able to do in a long time.

And our stories aren't over yet. Every year we go back to the drawing board and answer the same questions that we did in our initial strategy session. What's remarkable is that our belief system about what is possible for us is changing as we see more and more progress and opportunities. We keep rediscovering how amazing the human body is, and how it continues to adapt the more you take care of it and challenge it (in a good way).

After the significant results in our individual wellness stories and improvement in performance, we decided to share what had we learned with others. Firstly, to help others avoid the kinds of mistakes we both made during our careers by sacrificing our health for career success. And secondly, to help them build and sustain optimal health to drive peak performance – not just at work, but in life generally.

That is how Wellnesstory was born.

PART TWO
THE FOUR DRIVERS OF HEALTH

At this point, you may be thinking, 'OK, I can relate to a lot of what you are saying in terms of my health suffering due to my work life, and it's great that *you* managed to get healthy and fit, but *I* simply don't have the time to figure all this out for myself. It's entirely too complicated. There's so much conflicting information out there, and, quite frankly, I am not that interested in all the details. I just want a solution that fixes my health issues and makes me super-focused and energetic again, without having to invest a lot of time.' We hear you. It might feel like mission impossible to cut through all the noise and get to the bottom of what really drives our health, our performance and, ultimately, what enables us to live our best lives.

But here's the good news: the process for achieving peak health and performance is actually relatively straightforward. It is not easy, but it's less complicated than you might believe.

You see, our health is largely influenced by the drivers that shaped us to be the dominant species on the planet. These drivers are mindset (how we perceive or approach a situation), nutrition (what and when we eat), movement (cardio, mobility and strength) and sleep (both quality and quantity). These four drivers still impact our bodies today, and they do this in *exactly the same way* they did when we were living on the plains of Africa some 200,000 years ago. The same internal evolutionary programme is running in our bodies at a cellular level, but the environment we live in has utterly changed.

Modern life is certainly much more convenient, but our lifestyle is so out of sync with the natural rhythms that shaped us that it is, quite literally, killing us. Our always-on culture rarely gives us a chance to destress as we used to be able to with the rest of the clan while recounting stories of the day around the campfire. It used to be a daily struggle to find enough food to sustain us; nowadays, an overabundance of food means our body barely has time to digest one meal before we slam it with another. While modern transportation modes get us to where we're going much faster, this means our physical bodies rarely need to move any more. And we used to have no alternative but to sleep after the sun went down, whereas artificial light now makes it possible to work (or check our social media) late into the night. All of this comes at a high price for our health.

The science is now clear that these modern conveniences are responsible for the growing epidemic of so-called 'lifestyle diseases', including obesity, cardiovascular diseases, type 2 diabetes, most cancers and even dementia (including Alzheimer's, which is sometimes referred to as 'type 3 diabetes'). There is a popular misconception that most of these diseases are largely hereditary, but that's not quite the case. Sure, our genes determine a lot of things, such as the colour of our eyes and how tall we are. However, when it comes to our health, the picture is much more complex.

We may inherit predispositions to certain diseases, but our gene expressions – which control whether we become sick or not – are not set in stone. Think of genes as switches that can be turned on or off depending on the input received through the environment. You are not guaranteed to get cancer just because it runs in your family.[6] By making healthy lifestyle choices, you can dramatically reduce the risk of contracting lifestyle diseases, including cancer. On the other hand, even if these diseases are not in the family genes (eg obesity or type 2 diabetes), you can still contract them through unhealthy lifestyle choices.

People have a tendency to assume that it won't happen to them. 'No, I won't be the one diagnosed with cancer or diabetes or dementia.' The reality is that by working in a highly dynamic and stressful environment, like the airline industry, we actually compound the risks by prioritising work and putting our health on the back burner. When we experience chronic stress, fatigue, brain fog, frequent headaches, other aches and pains, digestion problems, poor sleep and poor moods, we chalk them up to getting older, or the price we pay for having a successful career. However, these symptoms are early warning signs that our bodies and minds are out of sync with their natural rhythms. And, like a warning light in the cockpit, if we continue to ignore them, we may eventually end up with a catastrophic incident.

Most of us experience the ill effects our fast-paced corporate lifestyles have on our daily lives. A stressful and unhealthy lifestyle inarguably impacts our mindset, our relationships, and even our world view. It deteriorates our performance, whether or not we want to admit it, and we end up in a vicious cycle. Poor eating habits lead to brain fog, mood swings and low energy. Lower energy is demotivating when it comes to any kind of physical exercise. Poor quality and quantity of sleep compounds the problems further. When we don't sleep well, our response times, focus, and even ability to learn and remember new information are seriously impaired and our immune system is compromised.

On the flip side, as the graphic below shows, a healthy diet drives higher levels of energy in the body, which helps motivate us to move more and improves the quality of our sleep. This, in turn, drives a better mindset, which then motivates better performance in each of the other areas – leading to a virtuous upward cycle of health and performance.

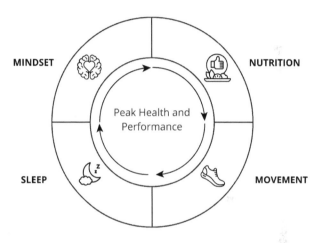

The four drivers of health

In the next four chapters, we will take the view of these drivers from 30,000 feet to consider the ways in which our modern lifestyle conflicts with our original evolutionary programming, and the problems this causes for our health. Don't worry, we won't get too 'sciencey', but to know where we're going, we need to understand where we came from. Understanding these evolutionary processes at a higher level will motivate us to make the relatively straightforward lifestyle changes that will bring our bodies and minds back into sync with the natural rhythms that helped shape us, which will allow our bodies to heal themselves and perform better.

We will be breaking down the science into understandable concepts that will, hopefully, resonate and provide you with your own 'aha' moments along the way. You can then internalise these and use them to motivate the necessary lifestyle changes. So, let's explore the four key drivers of health to better understand how we evolved, the importance of keeping our lifestyles consistent with our evolutionary programming, and the consequences when our lives are out of sync.

3
Mindset

Mindset is essential for setting our intentions and providing motivation for our goals. But what exactly do we mean by mindset, and why is it so important for our health? Broadly, mindset is a set of beliefs that shape the way we make sense of the world and ourselves. Our mindset is largely responsible for our relative success or failure in dealing with life's challenges and opportunities.[7] Having a growth mindset is the ability to take new information and ideas and incorporate them into our overall belief system to achieve our goals.

Having, or developing, this skill will be important on our journey towards peak health and performance. Understanding how our bodies evolved and the roles the four drivers of health play in our wellbeing will assist us to make better decisions and stay the course when things get difficult. We will also consider how stress and habit formation affect our overall mindset, and how each of these factors can either help or harm our health.

Fight or flight

Of course, it's impossible for us to really know what the mindset of our ancestors was and how they thought about themselves or their environment. What we do know is that life was not easy back then. There was the daily threat of being eaten by a predator or getting seriously injured trying to hunt prey, so it was undoubtedly stressful. Finding enough food to simply survive posed an everyday headache for hundreds of thousands of years. Archaeological records are full of examples of traumatic injuries in ancient peoples, including teeth and claw marks from predators and broken bones or cracked heads from hunting large animals. The fact that we survived as a species at all, caught between being prey and predator, is perhaps something of a miracle.

Thankfully, our bodies and minds evolved to deal with these extreme circumstances by developing the so-called 'fight or flight' response. This stress response is governed by our sympathetic nervous system, which triggers a cascade of hormones (primarily adrenaline and cortisol) that enable our bodies to quickly react to the stressor. The typical physiological responses are an increased heart rate and faster, shallower breathing. This provides increased oxygen to our major muscles. Our reflexes and senses (hearing, smell and optical focus) increase in intensity and our perception of pain reduces. Essentially, we become 'supercharged' to deal with an immediate and serious threat like an attacking predator or situations where we have to step up and deal with a big challenge. Normally, our body returns to its natural state 20 to 30 minutes after dealing with the threat.

Back then, the fight or flight mode was typically triggered in response to a serious life or death threat. Equally important, it was regularly counterbalanced by the parasympathetic (or 'rest and digest') mode, when the harsh levels of hormones subsided and the system returned to normal. And our ancestors had the most amazing ways of de-stressing by telling stories around the campfire at night or painting their deeds on the walls of their caves. We can only imagine how the poor victim who'd had a close encounter with a lion or who'd broken his spear while plunging it into a charging mammoth would have described the encounter in graphic detail, to the amazement of the audience. And everyone in the group would have felt a little calmer, a little more connected and grateful that their fellow tribesman had made it back in one piece. This sense of relief and the social interaction triggered the release of another hormone, oxytocin, the so-called 'love' or social interaction hormone, which can also induce anti-stress-like effects such as the reduction of blood pressure and cortisol levels.

Our ancestors were probably also more present in their daily lives. They couldn't afford to worry too much about the past or the future. They were simply surviving day to day, so they would have been focused on the priorities at hand rather than stressing over what might have been or what could happen in the future. In a way, it was a kind of mindfulness practice, before that was even a thing. This contributed to the overall balance of their stress response between their fight or flight and the rest and digest modes (the sympathetic and parasympathetic).

The always-on culture

What does this have to do with our own mindset in modern times? The problem is that with all our modern advances, our environment is vastly different to the one we evolved to live and thrive in. Our minds and bodies have struggled to adapt to the pace of change over the last century and, especially, the past few decades. Our stress response, which helped keep us alive in nature, is now permanently stuck in the 'on' mode and we rarely have a chance for one spike of adrenaline and cortisol to subside before another one happens.

To make things worse, our brain can't tell the difference between an attacking lion and modern-day stress such as bad traffic. Both are perceived as serious, so the body's reaction is equally forceful. Think of a situation when you've perhaps received an irate email from your boss. We bet that just thinking about it makes your heart beat faster. Your palms may get a bit sweaty and you might feel the need to take a few deep breaths to calm down. Your brain really can't tell the difference between a real and a perceived threat.

An undeniable accomplice in our always-on culture are our digital gadgets: our phones, laptops, iPads and other electronics that we increasingly rely on. Coupled with the still-too-common workaholic company culture, these make it easy and justifiable for us to work around the clock. Luckily, in the last decade an increasing number of countries are introducing the so-called 'right to disconnect' laws, which basically mean that no work emails are attended to after office hours.[8]

You might argue that aviation is a 24/7 business, so, as someone working in the industry, you are expected to always be 'on'. The truth is that as human beings we simply can't always be on. We need to recover sufficiently after a bout of stress. Constant overload of work results in declining performance. Paradoxically, chronic stress also hinders our ability to relax and recharge just when we need it the most. We will discuss the practical aspects of how to avoid this vicious cycle in Part Three, dealing with the TAKEOFF model.

Understanding mindset

As we discussed earlier, mindset is fundamentally how we perceive ourselves, our environment and others, and, consequently, how we respond to daily challenges. Over the past ten years, we have spent a significant amount of time trying to understand how our mindset impacts on our own health and performance. We've learned that our attitude shapes and drives our behaviour, and this largely determines our overall success. The next few paragraphs are a summary of what we have found to be the most relevant and impactful factors of mindset.

Perception is reality

Have you ever experienced an optical illusion – perhaps a visual puzzle or a piece of street art designed to 'trick' your brain? Perhaps you've heard a news story of someone who swears they have seen the image of Elvis in the foam on their latte? The point is that our individual concept of 'reality' is based on our perception. Perception can be defined as the organisation, identification and interpretation of the information we receive through our senses (ie vision, hearing, taste, smell and touch) to represent and understand the presented information or environment.[9] Our brains use perception to make sense of the information received through these sensory modes. We tend to think that our brains do a good job in this respect and that the images and other sensory data we receive present an accurate picture of the situation, like a video recording. However, as Dean Burnett explains in his fascinating book, *The Idiot Brain: A Neuroscientist Explains What Your Head Is Really Up To*, this is not the case.

'Many may think that what we perceive in our heads is a 100% accurate representation of the world as it is, as if the eyes and ears and the rest are essentially passive recording systems, receiving information and passing it on to the brain, which sorts it and organises it.'[10]

Instead, Burnett explains, the information we receive is actually partial, highly fragmented and often sifted out from a variety of other background noises. The brain then does an incredible job of combining this incomplete information with our memories and previous experiences of similar situations to form our 'reality'. This means that perception is based on our *subjective biases*, inherited from personal experiences or our upbringing, societal norms, etc. For example, in any sporting event, there will be winners and losers. If you're supporting the winning team, your perception will likely be that it was a 'good game'. However, if you're a losing supporter, your perception (and, therefore, your reality) is likely to be the opposite. Same result, two completely different realities.

This is where the problem arises for us when we're trying to build a mindset that is focused on building healthy habits. Our perceptions regarding what it means to be healthy will ultimately form our reality and govern the actions that we take, or fail to take, when it comes to our health. For example, if my perception is that being successful at my job means having to sacrifice everything, including my health, then that becomes my reality. If my perception is that being healthy actually enhances my performance, and therefore improves my success, then I will do everything to support that reality. I see things related to health and success in a completely different light.

Changing our perception, and therefore our reality, is possible, but it involves fighting against deeply ingrained experiences – ones that are reinforced each time we perceive a similar set of sensory events. Our brain tends to become biased towards such perceptions to reinforce our sense of 'reality'. We will talk more about the 'how' in changing our mindsets and perceptions in the TAKEOFF model. A big factor is simply being aware of the fact that we naturally make these associations and perceive the world based on incomplete sensory information and a large dollop of subjective interpretation. Often, that interpretation is based on incomplete facts and biased belief systems that no longer serve us.

Stress

As discussed earlier, we evolved to manage stress. We had to react to danger appropriately, hence the fight or flight response of our sympathetic nervous system. In a life or death situation, a number of nerve and hormonal signals kick in instantly: our mind zooms in on the danger to avoid all distraction and our body is flooded with adrenaline and cortisol to push our physical abilities to the maximum. Both of these hormones are produced in the adrenal glands and are absolutely vital to our survival.

Main stress hormones: Their roles and impact on the body

Cortisol	Adrenaline
• Increases blood sugar levels	• Increases heart rate
• Boosts the brain's ability to use glucose	• Elevates blood pressure
• Down-regulates non-essential functions such as digestion and the reproductive system	• Widens air passages
• Suppresses immune response	• Increases energy supplies

Source: Mayo Clinic, 'Chronic stress puts your health at risk'[11]

This is a highly efficient mechanism when dealing with acute stress (ie a sudden danger situation that lasts for a short period of time), but when stress becomes prolonged, the elevated adrenaline and cortisol levels can cause serious damage to the body. Chronic stress is associated with heart disease, depression, anxiety, memory and cognitive problems, difficulty sleeping, digestive issues, fatigue and weight gain.[12] The tricky part is that becoming sick due to stress happens gradually, and for a period of time we might not even be aware of it. It also doesn't immediately show up as full-blown depression or a heart attack. We might feel under the weather more of the time, catch the flu every time it's around, have trouble sleeping or are more moody or anxious than usual. If you are experiencing some, or all, of these symptoms, it might be wise to check with your doctor, as you may have issues with your adrenal glands.

While we usually think of stress as harmful, it is important to remember that some stress is actually necessary to grow and become more resilient. It is not about living life without any stressors – that is impossible – it's more about making sure that the stress is short-lived and that we can deal with it. We will discuss how to manage our stress in Part Three.

The power of habits

In his book, *The Power of Habit: Why we do what we do in life and business*, Charles Duhigg explains the evolutionary role of habits as a mechanism to save energy, enabling the brain to perform familiar tasks efficiently. He defines a habit as a loop of 'cue-routine-reward'.[13] Just think about how you brush your teeth in the morning. What is there to think about, you may wonder? I just brush my teeth and that's it. Exactly! You don't think about it. Our brain creates habits all the time. Once you've done something once, you will be able to do the same task faster next time, until it becomes so habitual that you don't need to think about it. The challenge with habits is to be mindful of the fact that not all habits serve our best interests. For example, taking the stairs in your office building instead of the elevator is a useful habit to have. It improves your circulation, works your muscles and gives your brain a well-deserved break. Eating at your desk, on the other hand, is a bad habit. Although we might think of it as an efficiency measure, we are not great at multitasking. We won't digest properly and we will probably shovel down more food than we actually need. Our brain is not designed to multitask. In fact, multitasking is associated with lower performance and reduced focus.[14]

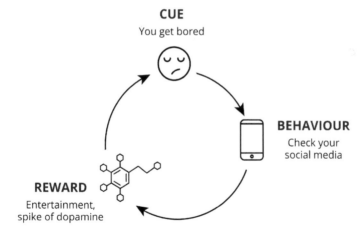

CUE
You get bored

BEHAVIOUR
Check your
social media

REWARD
Entertainment,
spike of dopamine

The habit loop (adapted from C Duhigg, The Power of Habit:
Why we do what we do in life and business[15])

Habits are powerful. They can help us to become better versions of ourselves, but they can also be harmful. Bad habits lower our work efficiency and productivity and ruin our health and our relationships. Think about behaviours such as interrupting, micro-managing, always being slightly late to meetings, taking work calls at all hours, eating convenient (junk) food to save time or having a glass or two of wine every evening to unwind. Now, we are not suggesting that having a glass of an amazing Albariño (or Cabernet Sauvignon) from time to time is a no-no, but realising that evening drinking has become a habit – possibly even a daily habit – is critical.

The question is: how to change a bad habit? The key, besides recognising the cue, is to be clear on the reward. What is it that we are trying to achieve with our habit? In the case of a glass of wine, it might be relaxation. Are there any other ways to achieve this? Maybe a walk with the dog, a nice bubble bath or listening to music would offer the same benefit. We will discuss how to tackle bad habits and build good ones in more detail in the TAKEOFF model.

Takeaways

- Mindset is largely responsible for our successes and failures in dealing with life's challenges and opportunities.

- Our ancestors survived due to their ability to respond to stress. The fight or flight response was triggered by serious life or death threats and periods of stress were balanced by periods of rest, recovery and time to recharge.

- Our brains cannot tell the difference between real danger and perceived danger (eg bad traffic or an irate boss). The same stress response is triggered by both.

- As a result of our always-on culture, we have lost our connection with ourselves and the world around us. We are living reactively rather than intentionally.

- The way we perceive the world around us creates what we believe to be reality, but perception is merely a collection of sensory information that is then combined with our individual experiences and memories.

- By being aware of the fact that perception is highly subjective, we can start to question our interpretation of the information we receive to make better judgements.

- We cannot avoid stress, but we can manage it once we become aware of our stressors.

- Habits are a powerful tool that allow us to perform certain tasks without thinking about them. They can either help us to become the best versions of ourselves or trap us in a half-life of bad health and underperformance.

4
Nutrition

Nutrition is a process of providing our bodies with all the necessary nutrients for health. The food that we eat nourishes our bodies and our brains. Eating according to our *natural human diet* is essential if we want to stay healthy, vibrant and live a long and productive life.

All species have their natural diets. For example, lions hunt large prey such as zebras or buffalos and, occasionally, some smaller animals and birds. Beavers are herbivores and eat aquatic plants and tree bark. All animals thrive on *their* natural diet, because they evolved to extract nutrients from the particular foods they eat.

So, what is our natural human diet? We like to put it this way: if you can hunt it, fish it or pick it in nature, it is part of the human diet. Let's unpack.

Feast and fast

Modern humans (*Homo sapiens*) have been eating what nature has to offer for millennia or, more precisely, for about 200,000 years. They had what we now refer to as a hunter-gatherer lifestyle, with a greater emphasis on the hunting than the gathering, because animals provided a more energy- and nutrient-dense food source than plants.[16] This process was, effectively, part of our evolutionary programming. We spent so much energy sourcing our daily sustenance that it made sense to maximise the outcome of our efforts. Our digestive system also evolved to be able to digest and extract the maximum amount of nutrients from an extraordinary variety of plants to ensure we survived in those times when the hunt was unsuccessful.

Food was strictly subject to availability, and was largely driven by the seasons and what was around at different locations. When there were abundant sources of protein around (ie during the hunting season), we ate as much as we could because there were no means of preserving the leftovers – at least not until we invented methods of preserving food, such as smoking, salting and freezing. And here is an interesting fact that will put your sugar cravings into perspective. We were programmed to crave sugar for the simple reason that fruit – the only source of sugar at the time[17] – was seasonal, and availability was strictly limited to a few weeks a year. Due to its rarity, and to ingest the maximum amount of nutrients and calories, we gorged on it until it was gone. Our bodies then converted the excess calories into stored fat to help us make it through the lean times of the dry African winter.

Speaking of lean times, when the herds migrated and the fruit and vegetables were out of season, there wasn't a lot to eat. It was those of us who had built up enough stored fat after a successful hunting season and by eating lots of fruit during the summer and autumn who were well prepared to survive the lean winter and early spring seasons and pass their genes on to the next generation. As humans, we developed the capacity to store much higher body fat reserves than any other primate species.[18] A relatively lean, healthy person carries about 100,000 kcal worth of fat at any given time – that's the equivalent of about thirty-five marathons.[19] Our bodies, being efficient machines, have evolved to use both sugar and fat as energy sources, depending on what foods are readily available and the needs of our bodies at the time. We are perfectly adapted to low or high energy demands and to dealing with times of abundance or caloric deficit. This is called 'metabolic flexibility', and we'll discuss it further later.

The fact that we have the capacity to use our own fat for energy enables us to endure long periods of fasting without losing alertness or focus. This was a critical necessity when we needed to stay on top of our game when hunting on an empty stomach. Before you say, 'That's it, I'm not reading any further. I am not going to fast; I simply cannot go hungry,' what if we told you that you already fast every single day, in accordance with your ancestral programming? The word breakfast literally means to 'break the fast'. You see, fasting doesn't necessarily mean going for days without food. We are programmed to fast for at least 12 hours to provide time for our bodies to self-clean and regenerate. This is a process called autophagy.[20] And, nobody brought us breakfast in bed back then. We had to get up and hunt or gather our breakfast first, so if you're not a breakfast person, now you know why.

The 'SAD' situation

So, what has changed since the time of the Flintstones? On a cellular level, absolutely nothing. Our bodies still thrive on our ancestral programme: consuming only those foods we can hunt and/or gather, eating as much as we can when food is available and having regular periods of fasting.

We also had to work extremely hard to procure our food, which meant expending energy and only eating after a successful hunting or foraging expedition, but nowadays, food is readily available everywhere and the effort of getting it hardly burns any calories. The food industry is a multi-trillion-dollar business that has only one objective: to sell us as much of their products as possible. They achieve their aim through ingenious marketing and food additives that make it difficult (if not impossible) for us to resist and so we eat way more than our bodies actually require. This so-called 'food' is rich in calorific values but poor in nutrients. Consequently, in our modern society, many people are overfed *and* undernourished at the same time. According to the World Health Organization:

- Worldwide obesity has tripled since 1975.

- 340 million children and adolescents aged 5-19 were overweight or obese in 2020.

- Between 2000 and 2016, there was a 5% increase in premature deaths caused by diabetes.

- Death from cardiovascular disease – the world's leading cause of death – is strongly associated with lifestyle choices.

- Diabetes was the ninth leading cause of death in 2019.

- At the time of writing this book, Alzheimer's is the fifth leading cause of death worldwide.[21]

Sad, isn't it? Speaking of sad, the standard American diet ('SAD') is high in added sugars, low in fibre and whole foods, high in saturated[22] and trans fats, high in sodium and is ultra-processed. This means that there is very little natural content left in it. This diet is causing alarming rates of obesity and diabetes in the US. And, while we like to point our fingers at the US, the rest of the Western world is not so far behind. The National Health Service in the UK estimated that the direct costs of treating obesity and its related comorbidities, in England alone, increased 12.7 times from £479.3 million in 1998 to £6.1 billion in 2015.[23]

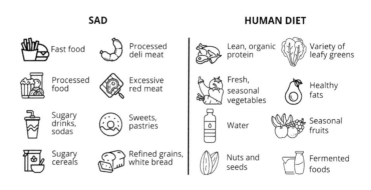

SAD		HUMAN DIET	
Fast food	Processed deli meat	Lean, organic protein	Variety of leafy greens
Processed food	Excessive red meat	Fresh, seasonal vegetables	Healthy fats
Sugary drinks, sodas	Sweets, pastries	Water	Seasonal fruits
Sugary cereals	Refined grains, white bread	Nuts and seeds	Fermented foods

SAD versus human diet

We cannot talk about the current state of the world's health without mentioning the numerous nutrition trends that, unfortunately, do more harm than good. For example, one of the biggest trends in the 1990s was eating 'little and often'. We were snacking the whole day and, if you were particularly health conscious, you opted for low fat options and margarine instead of butter. The common belief at the time was that eating small portions stimulated your metabolism. We now know that this is not how it works, as you will see below. Low fat was supposed to assist with keeping our fat intake to a minimum. This belief was fostered by the sugar industry and was nothing more than a clever marketing move to divert attention away from the actual harm that sugar does to our health. And, as margarine was plant based (despite being highly processed), it was considered much healthier than animal fat, which is not the case. Although there are still plenty of diet 'trends' out there, science is catching up fast and more and more of these unfounded claims are fast being debunked.

Understanding nutrition

The science of nutrition has really taken off in the past 20 years and we are learning tremendous amounts about how our bodies digest and absorb nutrients. As with the Mindset chapter, this is not intended to be a full or comprehensive overview of the field of nutrition. Instead, the aim of this section is to provide an introduction to three important factors that help us to figure out what and when to eat to stay healthy, fit and productive. There are many other crucial elements that shape our scientific understanding of how our bodies are impacted by nutrition. We have simply cherry-picked three, as we believe these will help you to better understand nutrition and stay on track with your practical application of the TAKEOFF model.

Healthy gut = healthy body and mind

The belief that illness stems from the gut is not new. In fact, the phrase 'All disease begins in the gut' is commonly attributed to Hippocrates, so it goes as far back as at least 2,500 years. Today, we know that perhaps not all, but certainly a large number of chronic diseases, such as arthritis, allergies, cancer, depression and anxiety, eczema, heart disease, autoimmune diseases, dementia (including Alzheimer's), obesity, type 2 diabetes, metabolic diseases (such as leaky gut), and many more are strongly linked to gut health.

Our gut is home to about 100 trillion bacteria.[24] According to *National Geographic*, the average human body has approximately 37 trillion cells, so the amount of our gut bacteria is about triple the number of our own cells.[25] These tiny organisms help us to break down the food we eat, absorb nutrients and protect us from toxins. The bacteria also work in a co-regulatory way with our immune system, 70% - 80% of which is located in our gut.[26] Our gut bacteria also significantly impact our brain health.[27] If everything is working as it should be and we have a wide variety of good gut bacteria, our immune system and our brain work well; if we have too little diversity and/ or predominantly unhealthy bacteria in our gut, we lose our ability to operate at peak performance and we also increase our risk of becoming chronically ill.[28]

As you can see, it is critically important to take good care of and feed our gut bacteria for optimal health.

In Part Three, we will discuss practical tips to keep a healthy and diverse microbiome. For now, it's enough to say that our modern ultra-processed diet, overuse of antibiotics, lack of sleep and sedentary lifestyle all contribute to the lack of diversity and diminishing numbers of good bacteria in our microbiome.

Sugar is making us sick and ageing us fast

Let's go back to our evolutionary design for a minute. As you learned earlier, we are fundamentally built to burn fat because, in our natural environment, carbohydrates were relatively rare and had a lower caloric value compared with meat.[29] Nowadays, we are bombarded with refined sugars and our bodies have become carb-dependent, which manifests in low energy and a constant sensation of hunger.

What happens when we eat carbohydrates? Depending on the nutritional quality of the carb, sugar will either be released into our bloodstream immediately, or more gradually. In response, our pancreas will secrete enough insulin to help the sugar make its way into our cells so it can be converted into energy. When the cells are full, some of the excess sugar will be stored in the muscles and liver. The problem is that our body can only store about 2,000 kcal as glucose (a soluble form of sugar). Once our glucose storage is full, any additional sugar is converted to fat. Boom! That's right. *Sugar makes you fat.* As long as we are overconsuming sugars (and most of us are), insulin will do its work and our body will store the excess sugar as fat. What's even more alarming than unnecessary excess weight is that a high-sugar diet causes cellular inflammation and accelerated ageing.[30]

Of course, as in most cases, quality matters and there is a big difference in the quality of carbohydrates. Complex carbohydrates such as fruits, vegetables, legumes and whole grains contain fibre and starch, both of which slow down the release and absorption of sugar into the bloodstream. Simple sugars such as refined sugar, fruit juices, fiizzy drinks, sweets, etc, are absorbed into the bloodstream immediately, causing an insulin spike and then a crash later. When the blood sugar suddenly drops, a signal goes to your brain that you need to replenish your reserves. This causes you to feel hungry again, which creates an endless cycle of craving and eating sugar-rich foods.

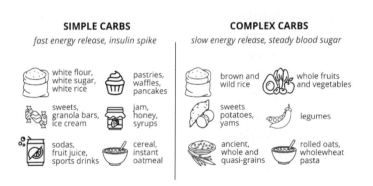

SIMPLE CARBS
fast energy release, insulin spike

white flour, white sugar, white rice

pastries, waffles, pancakes

sweets, granola bars, ice cream

jam, honey, syrups

sodas, fruit juice, sports drinks

cereal, instant oatmeal

COMPLEX CARBS
slow energy release, steady blood sugar

brown and wild rice

whole fruits and vegetables

sweets potatoes, yams

legumes

ancient, whole and quasi-grains

rolled oats, wholewheat pasta

Simple carbs versus complex carbs

Hormones play an essential role in our metabolism

Insulin is often called the master hormone because it plays an essential role in facilitating the transportation of nutrients into the cells and storing excess glucose, either in the muscles and liver or in our fat cells. A healthy level of insulin is beneficial as it protects the muscles from breaking down, promotes wound healing and aids bone formation.[31] Elevated insulin in the blood signals to the body that there is no need to release any of its own fat as energy is already available and abundant. Chronically high insulin levels can lead to insulin resistance and, eventually, type 2 diabetes. Insulin resistance[32] is associated with a number of serious conditions such as obesity, polycystic ovary syndrome (PCOS), certain cancers, cardiovascular diseases, non-alcoholic fatty liver disease and dementia.

Another key hormone worth mentioning when talking about nutrition is ghrelin, the hunger hormone. Ghrelin is mainly produced in our stomach and its function is to send signals to our brain to eat when the stomach is empty. The interesting thing about ghrelin is that it comes and goes in waves. In other words, you don't become hungrier and hungrier as time passes. If you are sceptical, try this next time you feel hungry. Distract yourself with something that you like to do, or go for a walk or drink a glass of water and see if you are still hungry in 5 minutes. (Having said that, certain people, especially those carrying excess weight, can be ghrelin sensitive. In other words, they feel hungry even when their ghrelin levels are lower.)

Leptin is the third hormone in this intricate system, and it is our so-called satiety hormone. It is produced in our fat cells and signals to our hypothalamus (the part of the brain responsible for metabolism) that we are satiated, or 'full'. The more leptin that reaches the brain, the fuller we feel. The problem is that we often eat either too fast or while multitasking (eating at the desk at work, anyone?), so we do not register this signal. As leptin is generated within fat tissue, levels tend to be low in lean people or in individuals who go on a calorie-restricted diet. Low levels of leptin are associated with low energy, and even depression and fertility problems (eg when the body deems it unsafe to reproduce because there aren't enough fat reserves to carry a baby to term). On the flip side, when the body is flooded with leptin, we become desensitised to the satiety signal leptin is trying to deliver and we keep eating even though our stomach is full.

Carbohydrates – especially refined simple carbs like sugar – shut down leptin receptors in our brain. This means simple carbs can make us insulin *and* leptin resistant at the same time – a double whammy that makes us fatter and fatter.

Our hormonal system is an amazing, beautiful and complex system and we will discuss how to optimise it using all four drivers of health in Part Three of the book.

Takeaways

- As humans, we evolved to eat a natural diet consisting of animals that we could hunt or fish, and plants that we could pick in season. Any other 'diet' does not make sense for our bodies.

- Feast and fast was, and still is, our natural rhythm and our bodies possess the unique ability to use our own fat as an energy source. Fasting also has numerous other benefits, including autophagy, blood sugar and mood regulation and enhanced brain performance.

- Our brains have been hijacked by the food industry, which has little concern for our health. The food industry's main goal is to increase sales. It achieves this through marketing and the use of artificial additives that make its ultra-processed 'food' almost impossible for us to resist.

- With 100 trillion bacteria living in our gut, we are more microbial than human. These tiny microbes are responsible for much more than our gut health. They impact our brain health and our immune system.

- Excess sugar in our diet makes us fat and is responsible for many lifestyle-related diseases.

- Our hormonal health is directly impacted by what, and when, we eat. Unsurprisingly, a modern carb-loaded diet wreaks havoc on our hormones.

5
Movement

If you have kids, you will probably have watched the cute Disney movie, *Wall-E*. It's about a future where we've totally destroyed the planet through overconsumption and corporate greed. (Sound familiar?) Luckily, most of the population is able to escape the dead planet via large, luxury cruise-type spaceships. During their extended journey in space, their every need is catered to, including these cool personal transportation devices where they don't need to walk anywhere, or even get out of them. Over time, this type of environment causes them to lose the ability to move by themselves. Unfortunately, as a society, we are rapidly heading towards that dystopian future (in more ways than one). The reality is that we are built to move. Our whole system and our health depend upon getting enough regular and varied movement.

The sedentary nature of our modern lifestyle is contributing to a sharp rise in lifestyle-related diseases as well as having an impact on our energy levels, our mood and, ultimately, our performance.

Move or die

It's difficult to imagine these days, but we used to be pretty low down the food chain when we were evolving in Africa. Back then, a lot of animals were bigger and faster than us and had a taste for our human relatives. As we began to descend from the trees and spend more time on the open plains, our bipedal design helped us to keep a closer eye on what was moving in the long grass and to get a better head-start as we ran for cover. As we started to develop more of a taste for meat ourselves, our ability to engage in scavenging and endurance hunting (essentially running down wounded prey until they gave up and collapsed) meant that we had access to better quality protein and fat. This fuelled stronger muscles and bigger brains.[33]

We were also constantly on the move. We followed the herds of large prey animals and were always on the lookout for other food sources to gather. Our bodies adapted accordingly. We developed longer, stronger legs to support our bipedalism and allow us to run fast over longer distances. Our larger brains enabled us to perform more complex tasks, including hunting for larger prey. The price of these evolutionary adaptations is that we constantly need to keep our bodies moving. As evolutionary biologist, Herman Pontzner, puts it, 'Exercise is not optional; it's essential... Our bodies evolved to require daily physical activity, and, consequently, exercise does not make our bodies work *more* so much as it makes them work *better.*'[34] Pontzner likens it to the evolution of certain species of shark. Their gills have adapted to allow water to flow over them and extract oxygen without the need for muscles to move the gills. This allows them to conserve energy, but the trade-off is that they have to keep moving, or they die![35]

Our movement patterns were also highly functional back then. We were either walking, running, jumping, climbing or carrying, and everything was done with an intention to get somewhere or to accomplish something. There was certainly no need to go to the gym because all of our movement requirements were satisfied by our daily activities. We also didn't spend a long time sitting (it was long before chairs were invented). Instead, we spent a lot of time squatting, which is an amazing position for building mobility and strength.

Although our ability to move was key in our evolutionary journey, it has now become critical to our overall health and vitality. Our evolution hard-baked the need for movement into our genes and this genetic imperative still lives within us.

Your chair is killing you

In modern times, unless you're an athlete of some kind, most forms of movement have become severely restricted as we have managed to engineer a lot of the need to move out of our lives. Take a typical day where we use the car to get to work and the elevator or escalator to our desks. We then sit in a chair for prolonged periods of the day – sometimes up to 8 hours or more. Typically, we don't even go for a walk at lunch time and, in the worst-case scenario, we eat at our desk – which also poses other issues from a nutritional point of view. In the evening, we're likely to sit at the table or in front of the TV for dinner, or endlessly scroll through our social media while sitting on a comfortable couch or recliner. Then we head for bed, usually without performing any kind of pre-bedtime wind-down or stretching. We don't even need to leave the house to get food any more. Our groceries can be delivered to the door (or we just call a delivery service for a pre-made meal – cutting out the need to even prepare it ourselves).[36] It's a long way from having to travel several kilometres to hunt down a gazelle or climb a steep cliff face to reach a beehive to access its sweet liquid gold. Now, we can do most things by simply reaching for our smart phones.

But why does this all matter? 'You need to move more.' We hear this mantra so often that it has become background noise. The World Health Organisation (WHO) have published fact sheets and guidelines urgently calling for people to move more, stating that over 5 million deaths per year could be avoided if we all simply did a minimum amount of physical activity.[37] They warn that the chronic lack of movement in the world is associated with a higher risk of all-cause mortality (ie increased risk of premature death from any cause), heart-related illnesses, growing levels of obesity (and all its associated health issues), type 2 diabetes and various forms of cancer.

On the other hand, increased physical activity dramatically reduces the risk of these problems, as well as providing a number of additional health benefits, for example:

- Preventing and managing noncommunicable diseases such as cardiovascular diseases, cancer and diabetes

- Enhancing thinking, learning and judgement skills

- Improving overall wellbeing

- Reducing the risk of all-cause mortality

- Reducing the risk of cardiovascular disease mortality

- Reducing incidents of hypertension

- Reducing incidents of site-specific cancers (bladder, breast, colon, endometrial, oesophageal adenocarcinoma, gastric and renal cancers)

- Reducing incidents of type 2 diabetes

- Improving balance and preventing falls

- Improving mental health (reduced symptoms of anxiety and depression)

- Improving cognitive health (reduces the risk of dementia and Alzheimer's)

- Improving sleep

- Helping to manage a healthy body composition[38]

That's an impressive list. There are no drugs out there that can come even close to these health benefits. And it doesn't need to involve a huge time commitment, either. The WHO recommends a minimum of 150–300 minutes per week of moderate-intensity physical activity (like walking or moderate-intensity swimming or biking), or just 75–150 minutes of vigorous-intensity level activity (like hill-walking or playing sports). That's the equivalent of around 20–40 minutes per day of moderate activity.

So, why are so many of us failing to meet even the minimum level of movement as per the WHO guidelines? Firstly, as we noted, a lot of the traditional forms of movement that would have been necessary before our modern times are now redundant. Secondly, we tend to have a lack of understanding of movement. What actually happens when we move? What happens if we don't move enough throughout our lives?

Finally, how can we manage to get enough movement in our daily lives to maintain a healthy lifestyle and perform at our best? We will look at the 'what' below, and the 'how' in Part Three.

Understanding movement

We now know that evolution has given us the gift of an amazing machine, capable of astonishing physical and mental feats. The price of this gift is the need to move – often and purposefully. But what does this actually mean on a physical and mental level? What difference does movement mean to our overall health and longevity in the longer term?

Movement changes your body

You will probably be aware that working out with weights can make your muscles grow, but most of us don't really understand the physiology behind this miracle of adaptation. We often associate muscle building with vanity and something that only body-builders do. There are also a whole lot of other changes going on in the body when we place it under stress. We change in radical ways: from our heart and blood vessels (cardiovascular system) and the capacity of our lungs (pulmonary system) to our muscles, but also, our joints, and even our bones, get stronger. Your body is a machine that changes to meet the challenges it faces. The more you challenge it, the more it adapts to meet these higher demands. Here are some specific examples of physical changes and adaptations:

- **Cardiovascular system:** When we exercise vigorously for an extended period, the muscles in our heart become stronger to pump harder and deliver more blood and oxygen to our muscles. We also grow more blood vessels around our muscles to deliver the oxygen more efficiently. Even the volume of our blood increases to carry more oxygen.

- **Pulmonary system:** Although this system is mostly made up of the lungs, it also includes our nasal cavity and windpipe (pharynx, larynx and trachea). This system is responsible for breathing. Oxygen is pulled into our lungs and oxygen is absorbed into our bloodstream through diffusion. Carbon dioxide (a waste product of metabolism) is transported out of the returning blood and breathed out of the lungs. The main adaptations to the pulmonary system are an increase in the number of blood vessels in the lungs to increase the volume of oxygen into the blood (and carbon dioxide out of the blood), and the muscles around your lungs strengthening to increase the depth and frequency of breathing.

- **Muscles:** There are different kinds of muscles in the body, but exercise affects mainly the skeletal muscles (ie the ones responsible for movement). There are two main types of skeletal muscles (Types I and II) and they adapt in slightly different ways. The main adaptations again relate to an increase in blood vessels around the muscles to deliver more oxygen when they're working, and increasing the number of mitochondria[39] in the cells of the muscles. The other significant adaptation is the efficiency of the neurological signals between the brain and the muscles, which make the working muscles more efficient.

- **Bones and joints:** We're aware that our bones have the ability to repair themselves in the case of breakage, but we tend to think of them as being solid and unchanging. Bone is a living, constantly changing tissue. Similarly, joints, (ie the intersection between two moving bones) are constantly renewing and regenerating. Physical exercise strengthens both bones and joints in the same way that challenging our muscles makes them stronger.

The adage 'Use it or lose it' is extremely relevant when it comes to our physical bodies. Our critical systems (cardiac and pulmonary), as well as our muscles, bones and joints, all rely on adequate movement to keep them healthy. Their ability to adapt and perform better is remarkable, but only if we use them.

Movement makes you smarter and happier

Along with the physical adaptations and increased physical performance, movement and exercise also impact on the function and performance of our brains.[40] Like our muscles (and every other organ in our bodies), our brains rely on blood flow for the delivery of oxygen and nutrients. As discussed above, physical exercise causes several adaptations in the circulatory and pulmonary systems that lead to higher volumes and more efficient delivery of oxygen and other nutrients to the cells, including brain cells. Physical activity also causes the release of certain hormones, including dopamine, serotonin and endorphins, which contribute to a better mental state. Dopamine is linked to your body's reward system. Endorphins are involved in the 'runner's high' phenomenon and are thought to encourage the body to continue to engage in physical activity, so they are important when forming healthy habits in this area.

Physical activity is also a highly effective stress management tool in that it acts as a distraction from stress. It is difficult to perform a vigorous workout and think about work related tasks, etc. Being mindful during exercise (ie noticing what's going on in your body and also focusing on your breath) increases the benefits even further.

Movement: The best anti-ageing pill

We all know people who have become old before their time. They become frail and weak and even appear older than they are, with premature wrinkles and sallow skin. Often, it is due to an unhealthy lifestyle, including a bad diet, smoking and/or drinking excessively. Added to this is the likelihood of a sedentary lifestyle. These unfortunate people will also tend to become less sharp as their cognitive function declines ahead of its time. The ageing curve below illustrates the trajectories for ageing and performance based on whether we stay relatively active as we age, or adopt an increasingly sedentary lifestyle and don't do enough physical activity.

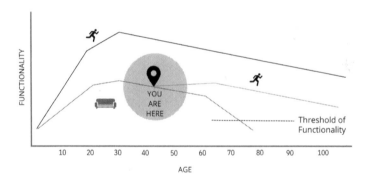

The ageing curve (adapted from A Friedlander, Exercise Physiology short course, Stanford Center for Health Education, 'Aging curve', Figure 1, Module 2)

What this curve demonstrates is that by maintaining an active lifestyle throughout the course of our lives, we can remain fully functional and healthy in later life. It also means that we will perform better, both physically and mentally, at each stage of our life. The impact of the more sedentary lifestyle, as shown with the lower curve, is that we will likely become 'functionally disabled' (see the so-called 'threshold of functionality' in the chart) at some stage in our lives. Mental function is also directly linked to physical movement (eg improved blood flow to the brain and improved neuroplasticity) and a lack of sufficient movement leads to lower cognitive function and a higher risk of dementia.

Not a pretty picture. On a positive note, if we increase our level of physical activity at almost any stage in our lives, we can push the curve out to avoid functional disability and live a fully functioning life until we, hopefully, pass away peacefully in our beds at a ripe old age. Our bodies are not only remarkably adaptable, they are also extremely resilient and have the power to regenerate and 'heal' themselves from years of abuse.

JIM'S STORY

Discovering the ageing curve was a major game-changer for me. I always had the impression that physical and mental decline are inevitable as we age, and there is little we can do to slow them down. Although fairly active earlier in my life, I had seriously let myself go in my thirties and forties and was convinced that my weight gain, muscle loss, aches and pains, and constant brain fog were just down to getting old and there wasn't much I could do about them. However, finding the ageing curve motivated me to think again and to start reversing some of the impact of poor lifestyle and lack of sufficient movement. Now, my focus is on how I can build as much of a reserve in terms of muscle mass, bone density and strengthened joints to avoid functional disability later in life. I also want to reduce my risks of contracting a cognitive illness.

Takeaways

- As humans, we evolved to constantly move. It was either eat or be eaten. Walking and running made up the majority of our physical movement but we were also engaging in other functional movements such as climbing, lifting, squatting, etc.

- This need to move has been baked into our genetic design and remains critical to our health. It's not an option. It's an imperative.

- Unfortunately, we have engineered most of the need for movement out of our lives and it can be challenging to get a minimum level of physical activity to keep us healthy.

- The WHO has set some reasonable guidelines for minimum levels of movement, but many of us are failing to meet even these.

- The impact of this failure to move is dire, with greater numbers suffering from increased risk of lifestyle-related illnesses and functional disability.

- Getting sufficient exercise dramatically reduces the risk of these diseases.

- Our bodies and minds are remarkably adaptive, and exercise improves the efficiency and performance of both.

- Movement is the ultimate anti-ageing tool and can keep us functional and healthy late into our lives.

6
Sleep

Sleep is probably the least understood of the four drivers of health. It is often viewed as a time of inactivity, or worse, as a waste of time. Through major leaps in the science of sleep, we now understand that it is foundational to our health. Sleep helps us to recharge our batteries, but it is also essential for almost all aspects of our physical, mental and emotional lives. In our always-on world, sleep is often viewed as something to be limited in the name of efficiency. As we will see in this chapter, such thinking is based on a false economy and actually damages our health and seriously undermines our performance. Sleep can be a superpower that energises, renews and enables us to operate at our peak capacity. A lack of adequate sleep can leave us in a fog of irrationality and low energy and put us at higher risk of many lifestyle-related diseases.

Night and day

Picture this. It's around 200,000 years ago. It's late in the evening and the sun is setting. It's been a long and active day. You spent a lot of it hunting a large animal and then carrying it several kilometres back to camp. You're tired. As you sit by the warm campfire after eating a nutrient-packed meal and trading stories with your fellow tribesmen, it's time to wind down for the day. You welcome the onset of sleep as it seems to recharge you for the following day. There are times where you've had to 'stretch the day' by delaying sleep, perhaps because of an all-night hunt when the moon was full. But eventually, once the hunt was over and the adrenaline and cortisol subsided, you passed out. In those situations, you would have had an opportunity to recover over the next few days, maybe even napping during the day if the hunt was particularly successful. Your sleep largely followed the cycle of the sun: you slept when the sun went down, and you awoke when it rose, ready for the day ahead.

We seem to struggle with this concept today. Why is one-third of our lives spent on such a seemingly unproductive activity? Can it be that sleep is an evolutionary misstep? You may be surprised to know that the origins of sleep are now understood to date back to deep in evolutionary times. A study on melatonin production (the hormone that controls the onset of sleep) found a similar process to humans in marine organisms that haven't changed much in the past 700 million years.[41] Despite this evolutionary imperative, we continue to push the boundaries in relation to limiting the amount of sleep we get.

I'll sleep when I'm dead

You've probably experienced this bravado around cutting sleep in your own career. Sleep is almost considered to be a weakness, a waste of time and something to be reduced – given that we can't avoid it entirely. You've probably pulled all-nighters on several occasions, either during college or for work, due to the urgency of some deadline or other. In our hyper-competitive world, there is huge pressure to look for 'efficiencies' everywhere and sleep is one of the usual candidates. While it is possible to go without sleep for an extended period of time, the impact on our bodies and minds is considerable and long-lasting, particularly if we don't have the opportunity to adequately recover afterwards.[42]

JIM'S STORY

I recall working on a major transaction involving a certain Italian national airline. The deal was complex, with a lot of parties involved. As with a lot of things in Italy, it was also difficult to nail down the final details. There was a lot of sacrificing of sleep during that transaction, but I recall one particular all-nighter. My morning had started at 7am, with negotiations beginning at 8am. Discussions were intense, with lunch and dinner (sandwiches!) eaten in the conference room. As the hours wore on, it looked like the deal was in real jeopardy. The parties were entrenched and it took considerable effort to get everyone over the line. The commercial discussions finally ended around 2.30am the following morning. Once the commercial people had left the room, I continued drafting the final points with the other lawyers. We finished just minutes before the press conference at 2pm, when the two CEOs announced the deal. But we still had a lot of clean-up work to do, so I ended up working until the celebratory dinner at 9pm that evening. I finally made it to bed at about midnight. In total, I had been awake for over 40 hours. In fact, the only thing that made it possible for me to stay awake during that time was consuming copious amounts of Italian espresso (more on the impact of caffeine on sleep later). I managed to eventually get some sleep that night, but it was not good quality sleep and I felt as though I had been hit by a large train the next day. The effects were akin to really bad jet lag and lasted for several days.

We've all had similar experiences in the name of 'getting the job done' despite the cost to our sleep, but were the outcomes optimal? Some of the effects of sleep deprivation are that our judgement and response times are seriously impaired, as well as our ability to take in and process new information. We also become less rational and more emotional, and so our decision-making becomes impaired. There have been several case studies done on the effects of sleep deprivation and response times while driving. The Institute of Medicine (US) Committee on Sleep Medicine and Research found that almost 20% of all serious car crash injuries in the general population are associated with driver sleepiness, independent of alcohol effects.[43] We may be able to function based on a certain level of sleep deprivation, but our performance will be significantly suboptimal, and even dangerous, in certain situations.[44]

Perhaps the more worrying side of the sleep deprivation coin is that, despite more people realising the importance of sleep, they are finding it increasingly difficult to actually get a good night's sleep. In its 2021 Global Sleep Survey,[45] Royal Phillips, a global leader in health technology, found that only around 55% of participants were completely or somewhat satisfied with their sleep. Stress is a major inhibitor of sleep. Cortisol from the stress response makes you stay awake but, ironically, you may feel very tired at the same time.[46] Even in 'normal' circumstances, our modern lifestyle makes it difficult to get good sleep. The resulting 'sleep deprivation epidemic', as it has been called by the Centers for Disease Control and Prevention (CDC), has been linked to an elevated risk of premature death or contracting one of a number of lifestyle-related diseases.[47]

As in other areas of our lives, such as nutrition and movement, the natural rhythms that dictate how and when we sleep have become so thoroughly disrupted that we struggle to get the quantity and quality of sleep we require for optimal health.

Understanding sleep

So, what's your perception of sleep? Is it something that you can't avoid or is it a crucial element in your health and performance? If we understand the 'why', it is more likely that we will prioritise this essential element of our health.

Why we sleep

In his highly popular book, *Why We Sleep: The New Science of Sleep and Dreams*, neuroscientist and sleep specialist Matthew Walker sets out a comprehensive explanation of why we sleep, as well as the health risks of not getting enough sleep. According to Walker, 'Sleep is the single most important thing we can do to reset our brain and body health each day.'[48] Far from being a waste of time and something we should limit, sleep affects every system of our body and brain – from repair and regeneration of tissue, to supporting our immune system, to moderating our hormones and keeping us on an even keel in terms of our emotions. It even aids us in learning and memory and boosts creativity.

Although scientists don't have all the answers yet on *why* we sleep, these are the main current theories on how sleep impacts us from a health and performance point of view:[49]

- **Cellular restoration**: Sleep provides an opportunity for the body to restore itself – something that is more difficult to do when our bodies are awake and active.

- **Brain function:** During sleep, the toxic by-products from energy production in the brain that have built up during the day are removed.[50] Sleep also allows us to process and store memories.

- **Emotional wellbeing:** During sleep, brain activity increases in areas that regulate emotion, thereby supporting healthy brain function and emotional stability.

- **Weight maintenance:** Sleep helps to regulate the two main hormones controlling hunger: ghrelin and leptin. An imbalance in these hormones can cause weight gain.

- **Proper insulin function:** It is thought that sleep may help to regulate insulin in several ways, which can prevent insulin sensitivity and type 2 diabetes.

- **Boosts our immunity:** When we sleep, our bodies produce antibodies and immune cells that help support our immune system.

- **Heart health:** Sleep is essential for heart health and a lack of it can lead to high blood pressure, elevated cortisol levels and increased inflammation, among other conditions.

Hopefully you are now both in awe of the power of sleep and inspired to start sleeping more to improve your health and performance.

A good night's sleep starts in the morning

You might be familiar with the term 'circadian rhythm' and probably even associate it with sleep. Most people are not fully aware of what this delicate ballet of hormones actually is, and how important it is for our health and for getting a good night's sleep. 'Circadian' comes from the Latin *circa* ('around') and *dies* (a 'day'). This refers to the fact that the circadian rhythm is a cycle of about 24 hours.[51] The cycle involves an interplay between two hormones: the stress hormone, cortisol, and the sleep hormone, melatonin. The production of melatonin in the evening is what triggers the onset of sleep, and a buildup of cortisol and other hormones in the early morning is what causes us to wake up. The production of these hormones is governed by receptors in our eyes which trigger our pituitary gland to produce the necessary hormones.[52]

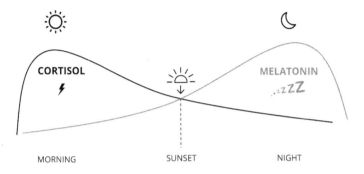

Human circadian rhythm

One of the biggest challenges for getting good sleep in our modern world is that these light signals have become drowned out by the light pollution from artificial light. One of the worst offenders is our device screens. The blue light wavelength emitted from them (and other modern sources of light such as LED bulbs) mimics the light of the rising sun. Think of it this way. It's time to wind down for sleep. You've had your camomile tea and put on your favourite jammies. You climb into bed, but you can't resist the urge to check your emails or your social media account(s) one last time. You stare at the screen and scroll through emails and posts for half an hour or more, probably unaware of time passing. Then you try to go to sleep, but you've just given your brain a signal that it's morning: time to get up! Instead of producing melatonin, you've just told your body to produce cortisol (which, if you remember, is also the stress hormone). Now, not only will it take you longer to get to sleep but, more importantly, the quality of your sleep will also suffer.

Sleep stages

The other important element of sleep (after the circadian rhythm) are the various stages of sleep we go through each night. We're all familiar with the terms deep and REM ('rapid eye movement' or dream phase) sleep, but did you know there are actually five stages of sleep? In addition to REM, there are four types of 'non-REM', or 'NREM'. Although all of the stages are important, from a health and performance point of view, the two most important ones are deep and REM. Like the circadian rhythm, the sleep stages are a delicate dance performed each night, and the amount and timing of the different stages are critical to whether we wake up rested and energised or feeling tired and drained. Typically, there are five 'cycles' per night, and we cycle through each of the above sleep stages to varying degrees. This assumes we get about 7-8 hours of sleep at night. Anything shorter and we can miss a cycle entirely or wake up in the middle of one, neither of which is a pleasant experience.[53]

The illustration below explains our sleep stages. Importantly, there is a push-pull relationship between REM and deep sleep where we experience a greater amount of deep sleep earlier at night (usually between 11pm and 4am) and a greater amount of REM sleep later on (between 4am and 7am). This is relevant for the timing of when we sleep. Going to bed after midnight means sacrificing a lot of deep sleep, whereas getting up for that hideously early morning flight means sacrificing REM sleep. Both have important functions: deep sleep is responsible for overall regeneration and restoration of our systems and cells, whereas REM is important for cognition, critical thinking and emotional regulation.

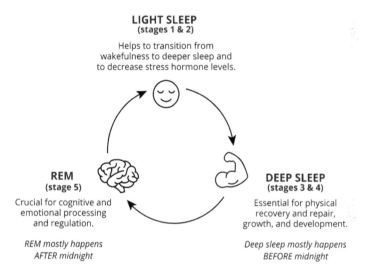

LIGHT SLEEP
(stages 1 & 2)

Helps to transition from wakefulness to deeper sleep and to decrease stress hormone levels.

REM
(stage 5)

Crucial for cognitive and emotional processing and regulation.

REM mostly happens AFTER midnight

DEEP SLEEP
(stages 3 & 4)

Essential for physical recovery and repair, growth, and development.

Deep sleep mostly happens BEFORE midnight

The five stages of sleep

Balancing our sleep timing to ensure that we have enough of the types and stages of sleep is important to overall health. The length of time we spend in each of these stages will also influence how we perform during the day. Although it is difficult to achieve the perfect balance between the various sleep stages and cycles, the closer we can get to this balance, the more we are leveraging the superpower of sleep. We will discuss more in the TAKEOFF model about how we can achieve a better quantity and quality of sleep.

Takeaways

- Sleep is one of the oldest evolutionary adaptations and is common to all animals. We can't avoid it and trying to do so is deeply damaging for our health.

- Even when we want to get a good night's sleep, it can be difficult due to our modern lifestyles.

- Sleep is governed by our circadian rhythm which, in turn, is influenced by the light of the rising and setting sun.

- Modern artificial light sources (particularly screens from mobile phones and other devices) are seriously disrupting our circadian rhythms and, therefore, our sleep.

- Our sleep cycles and the interplay between our REM and non-REM stages of sleep determine the quality of our sleep. Getting the right balance of each is critical to our overall health and performance.

PART THREE
THE TAKEOFF MODEL

A re you still with us? It's a lot of information to get your head around, but hopefully the overview of the four drivers of health in Part Two has provided you with some powerful 'aha' moments and that you're eager to learn how you can create a healthier lifestyle and improve your overall performance. As the old saying goes, 'Knowledge is power … but only when you use it.' This is where the rubber meets the runway.

To recap what we've covered so far. Humans evolved to become the dominant species on the planet, after spending the majority of our evolution being preyed on by larger predators. Part of our success was our ability to adapt to new environments in relation to our diet and movement patterns. We thrived on a wide variety of plants and animals, which we ate seasonally as we moved from place to place on our journey. Movement was a critical factor in our success. We walked and ran everywhere. We lifted, carried, climbed, squatted and played constantly. And then we slept and allowed our bodies and minds to recover and be restored.

A curious and determined mindset helped us to continuously push the boundaries of our existence. This has led to our modern world and all of our amazing developments and achievements but, ironically, a lot of our modern conveniences are overriding the natural rhythms that our bodies still need to be healthy and to perform to the best of our ability. For example, our cycles of eating and fasting, once dictated by the seasons, are now completely disrupted.

We've talked a lot about the consequences of our modern lifestyle on our health, especially regarding lifestyle-related diseases. But equally important is the impact they have on our daily lives: low energy, brain fog, moodiness, anxiety, depression, pains and aches. These colour the way we live and impact our mindset. We normalise our ill health, our underperformance, our 'half-lives'. We chalk it up to the price of success or having a busy, stressful life. We just have to 'man up' (or 'woman up') and power through it.

But here's the good news. We can live healthy, happy lifestyles *and* perform at our highest levels. Athletes realise this. They look for every half-percent improvement in their nutrition, movement patterns and sleep. They even have mindset coaches to improve their mental resilience. This principle doesn't just apply to athletes. They have simply rediscovered the reality that we have to work at our health to improve our performance. Our natural environment used to dictate a healthy rhythm of life, but now we have to actively recreate it to be healthy and happy. It is truly inspiring to watch the results of these efforts in the field of sports. Every year there are new world records being set in every discipline. We haven't yet found the limits of our abilities.

So, why not you? What's stopping you from being the healthiest, most successful version of yourself? We can probably anticipate your answers, because we were there and still struggle with the same challenges in our own busy lives. A lot of it is down to time: 'I don't have time. My schedule is way too busy to even start thinking about how to change all these things you're talking about.' Energy levels, maybe? 'I'm too tired to even contemplate doing a workout or trying to plan for healthy eating.' And sleep? 'I'd love to sleep more, but lack of time and then not being able to sleep when I finally do go to bed are the problem.' Mindset? 'I rarely think about it. I just get up and go. I'm so busy and stressed to even think about change.'

If this sounds familiar, then welcome to the TAKEOFF model. We've specifically designed it for busy airline executives and their teams, although it's applicable to anyone who wants to take back their health and get back on top of their game, but don't know where and how to start. Factoring in your busy schedule, TAKEOFF is designed so that you take small, incremental actions in each of the four drivers of health to build a virtuous, upward spiral of health, which then improves both your physical and mental performance. By taking these small actions over an extended period of time, you will start to change your habits. Once something becomes a habit, it is much easier to sustain because you will do it largely without thinking.

Each perceivable improvement in any one area boosts your motivation (mindset), which creates an updraft for a further cycle of improvements. The time you invest in each small improvement is paid back manyfold in terms of your overall health and performance. It will seem like you have more time, simply because you are able to better concentrate/focus and, therefore, use your time more efficiently.

There are seven elements in the TAKEOFF model. We've summarised each of them below for a brief overview:

1. **Turn off autopilot:** Have you ever noticed that you feel incredibly busy during the day, but can't remember what you've done in the evening? The reality is that most of us operate on autopilot most of the time. We're so overwhelmed by the pace of modern life that we go into survival mode.

The first step in building a sustainable healthy lifestyle is to turn that autopilot off and start to become aware of, and intentional about, our actions and habits.

2. **Address your stress:** We have a tendency to stress about stress. Stress is, of course, real and can be deeply damaging to our health, but stress is also what helped us to survive and thrive as a species. We need stress to motivate us and propel us to new heights. Acknowledging and managing that stress is key to our health and performance.

3. **Know your 'Why':** Changing the habits of a lifetime is challenging and requires commitment and a clear understanding of why you're doing it. Having a strong Why, or a rock-solid motivation for making these changes, is critical. It will help to anchor your commitment and serve as a reminder when things get tough.

4. **Eat your way to health:** Nutrition is the bedrock of our health. Food is not just fuel. It also provides the building blocks for our bodies. Eating healthy means a healthy body and mind. Reconnecting with our 'natural diet' and providing the body the nutrients it needs is life-changing.

5. **Overhaul your movement:** We evolved to move. Physical movement affects every system in our bodies, including our brain function and emotional

wellbeing, but we have essentially engineered the need to move out of our lives in the name of convenience. We need to increase our normal daily movements like walking, climbing the stairs, etc, and also balance this with more formal exercise, including cardio, mobility/flexibility and strength exercises.

6. **Fix your sleep:** Sleep is our little-known superpower. It is crucial for our health and also supercharges our performance. Maximising both your quantity and quality of sleep will radically shift your health and performance.

7. **Fasten your seat belt!** This is going to be a fun, but challenging, ride. There will be some turbulence along the way, but we're strapped in and are committed to this lifelong journey.

Over the next few chapters, we will unpack each of these elements and explain how they work and how you can start to implement them in your daily life. To help you on your journey, at the end of the book, we have included a link to exercises, checklists, workbooks, techniques and other useful resources, including the first six weeks of our signature TAKE-OFF programme.

Are you ready for TAKEOFF?

7
T – Turn Off Autopilot

Have you ever driven halfway somewhere only to realise that it wasn't where you wanted to go at all? We bet you have. Your mind kicks into 'autopilot' so that you can focus on something else, like worrying about that work deadline you might miss or the kids' upcoming playdate that you need to bake healthy muffins for. Studies show that we are on autopilot almost *50% of the time*. (Except when we're making love. Apparently, we need to be a bit more focused for that!)[54]

Become aware

How we perceive the world around us, discussed in Chapter Three, is also a kind of autopilot. Our reality is shaped by information we receive through our five senses, but is then interpreted via our previous experiences and usually highly subjective beliefs. If we are unaware that this is happening, we are probably taking actions without really thinking about them and letting our subjective past experience dictate our future actions.

Being on 'autopilot' has a specific meaning in aviation terms. It's a piece of technology that controls the plane and allows the pilots to focus on other tasks without compromising safety. Crucially though, when things get a bit complex, like flying through a storm or for a particularly difficult landing, the pilot takes over again. Similarly, when it comes to us being on autopilot, it means that we can do something without having to think about it. And therein lies the problem. Autopilot is beneficial when we are performing habitual tasks in a familiar environment because it saves energy and frees up mental resources. It becomes a problem when we spend a significant part of our lives doing things habitually (ie without thinking about them). We sacrifice a great deal of control over our lives.

This pattern often happens when we are in survival mode: our lives become so stressful that our unconscious mind starts to take shortcuts, which is what habits essentially are. Take the example of one of the most common office habits: the muffin/coffee combo between 3pm and 5pm. When we have an energy dip in the afternoon, we don't consciously think about what the best option for our health and performance might be. We generally take the quick, easy way – sugar and caffeine – to keep us going. This makes sense in the short-term but has serious medium- and long-term health consequences.

When we are trying to solve a complex issue at work, we should ideally start by taking a step back and looking at the big picture. Doing so forces us to turn off our autopilot, which is counterproductive in situations where there is volatility, uncertainty, complexity and ambiguity (VUCA[55]). We need to be completely present and give 100% of our attention to the challenge in front of us. We need to consciously widen our focus to see as many details as possible to gain insights into potential solutions that we might not see otherwise.

In the case of our health, stepping back and being intentional about our actions is just as important. We need to acknowledge the potential issues that we may be facing and connect the dots before we make a plan to change. This is not a one-time exercise. You will find that becoming more aware and intentional requires some practice. Luckily, mindfulness is a tool that helps us to do just that.

The practice of mindfulness

Mindfulness has gone mainstream in the last few decades. There is an increasing amount of research that demonstrates the benefits of practising mindfulness for corporate executives. These include better focus, efficiency, creativity, resilience and relationships.[56]

Many people associate mindfulness with inner reflection and profound internal experiences, when, in reality, mindfulness is as simple as thinking about what you're doing *as* you are doing it. To be a bit more scientific, mindfulness is about present moment attention, metacognition and non-reactivity. It's about the ability to pay attention to what is, and how it is, without judging it. It's about creating space for a response rather than a reaction to whatever the situation might be. In other words, being mindful in the moment increases our awareness of the situation at hand. It takes us out of habitual action. It can also switch us from being in a reactive, fight or flight mode into a calmer, reflective parasympathetic mode where we can reflect on the full picture before taking more informed action.

In our current day and age, being mindful doesn't come naturally for most of us. To be able to be more present in the moments when we need it the most, we need to train our 'mindfulness muscle' outside of those situations. There are different types and forms of mindfulness practice.

Formal practice

This is essentially what we refer to as meditation. Depending on the type of meditation, this might involve focusing on the breath, becoming aware of the body's sensations and thoughts, or chanting, to mention just a few. Contrary to popular belief, meditation does not involve having to clear your mind of any thoughts or some highly spiritual experience. These common myths are what turn many people off the practice. Instead, meditation is about giving your mind a break. Thoughts will inevitably come and go, but this is an opportunity to simply observe them dispassionately and then let them pass. Like anything in life, the more you practise meditation, the more natural it becomes and the greater the benefits you will reap.

Informal practice

This can be incorporated into our daily lives with little additional time commitment. There are a number of simple, but highly effective, mindfulness techniques. Below are just two that we use regularly:

- **Take a minute to pause:** For example, before a difficult conversation, a meeting, big speech, etc. By taking, quite literally, one minute to just focus on your normal breathing, maybe even counting your breaths and becoming aware of any physical sensations in your body, you shift your focus from what can be a stressful emotional state to a very different one: the physical domain. You will feel immediate relief as a calmer and more confident state of mind emerges. Fair warning: if you are not prepared for the meeting, the one-minute mindfulness practice will not save you, but it will certainly make you feel more present and, hopefully, better able to succeed on the fly!

- **Mindful walking:** Walking naturally decreases cortisol levels and calms our nervous system. It's one of those activities that have multiple benefits across all of the drivers of our health. We recommend going for short ten-minute walks at least three times a day. While you walk, do a little exercise, try to switch on your different senses one after the other and take a few minutes to savour them individually. First, you may want to focus on the temperature and how it makes you feel. Then, shift your attention to the light: is it sunny or cloudy? How bright or dull is it? What colours do you see? Now focus on the sounds: how many can you hear? How loud or soft are they? You can continue with whatever comes to mind. Observe and walk, with full awareness of your body and your surroundings.

For optimal results, both forms of mindfulness practice should be a part of your daily life, but we have found that starting with the informal practice can ease you into the habit of mindfulness, which helps you to build your mindfulness muscle for a more regular formal practice. And for those of us who need quantifiable proof of the benefits before they will commit to meditation or mindfulness practice, several studies have now demonstrated how regular practice causes physical changes to the brain. One such study found a notable decrease in the size of the amygdala (the organ in the brain that controls fear and stress). Mindfulness makes us more resilient to stress.[57]

NATASA'S STORY

As Head of Corporate Communications and Public Affairs, I used to spend countless hours flying from one city to another, whether for press conferences or for meetings with regulators or other partners. While some of my colleagues spent most of this time writing emails and working on presentations and meeting memos, I felt like my brain needed a break from my laptop. I would use this time as an opportunity to refresh and refocus. I found flying to be a perfect time for some mindfulness practice, eg listening to a guided meditation or music or simply staring at the clouds. These activities relax our brains and rebalance our hormonal system. I'd arrive at my destination feeling more grounded and ready for whatever the day might bring.

Develop healthy habits

It's clear that having healthy habits is beneficial to our health and our performance, but if you've ever tried to replace a bad habit with a new, healthier one, you know how difficult it is. There is a lot more to be said about the topic of habit change, but for now, here are some principles that you can start applying in your life to see immediate results.

Take small steps

So, you know what to do, you've read all the science and are fully aware of what needs to be done. And yet, you don't do it. More often than not, the required change in our routine or behaviour is too big and it can feel overwhelming. For example, your goal is to run your first marathon. You probably won't start by trying to run the 26 miles (42 km) on day one, right? You will consider your current fitness level, adjust your nutrition and sleep and make a plan. You will start out small and build up gradually. In his book, *Slow Burn: Burn fat faster by exercising slower*, ultramarathon runner Stu Mittleman describes cases where he asks his clients to literally walk in the beginning as they prepare for their longer runs.[58]

Taking small steps *consistently* will allow you to build on a solid foundation as you progress towards your goal. And, most importantly, it will keep you on track and motivated to take further action. Think about it this way: swapping your store-bought fruit juice with a homemade green smoothie is a small change to your diet on any given day, but if you keep doing it, you will notice the positive impact on your mental state and waistline, and so you might feel inspired to start eating healthier overall.

Another great motivator, as we now know from understanding habits, is the power of reward. Set yourself small milestones and celebrate when you achieve them. Lost the first 2 kg of the goal of 10? Celebrate! Training for a marathon and completed your first 10 km run? Celebrate! Now, here is the trick. Celebrate with something that fits in with your goal.

In the case of a weight loss milestone, perhaps treat yourself to a massage, rather than a muffin. In the case of reaching a running milestone, you might reward yourself with a subscription to *Runner's World*. The trick is to do it consistently and one small step at a time. As you start to see results, it builds your motivation to take further small steps, and so on.

Create the right environment

We recently bought a CrossFit rower from somebody who rarely used it. Jim was over the moon. It was something that he'd wanted to get for some time to support his fitness goals. When we asked the seller why they were selling the rower, she said that they didn't use it much because, due to space restrictions, it was inconvenient to pull it out and then put it away after use. We put the rower in our outdoor fitness space, so every time we look out into the garden, it is literally inviting us to use it. Jim uses it almost every day.

For a long time, making green smoothies was a hassle for us. We had a relatively simple blender and often didn't have the right veggies in the fridge, but we were determined to start our morning with a nutrient boost instead of a shot of caffeine. So, we bought a Vitamix (top-end blender) that lives on our countertop, and set an order list from our grocery store on a weekly repeat. Result? Delicious, creamy smoothies every morning, without question and with no hassle.

Creating the right setup is key to forming habits because most of the cues come from our environment. Set it up right and you increase your chances of success. If you make it difficult for yourself, you will probably not enjoy it and, ultimately, fail to keep it up.

Find your tribe

This is probably the principle that we arrived at last, but it is invaluable. Surround yourself with people for whom your new behaviour, mindset and identity are the norm. A community of like-minded people will not only motivate you, but also boost your self-confidence and accelerate your progress. There are endless possibilities for tapping into the power of community and accountability, including sports clubs, Facebook groups or apps that have a form of progress tracking that can be shared with others. To benefit from the amazing power of this principle, remember that *any* community you join requires your participation.

JIM'S STORY

Natasa and I, like many busy executives, struggled to stay on track with our fitness goals. It was hard to establish a sensible, sustainable routine of physical activities that we actually liked. We tried a number of things, including running and personal trainers, but, somehow, there was almost no progress. A few months after we moved to Haarlem, we found CrossFit and decided to give it a go. We loved it. As opposed to other sports, CrossFit covers a range of movements and is actually fun to do. Even more importantly, we instantly found a community of like-minded people of different ages, professions, shapes and fitness levels all supporting one another. We feel bad if we have to miss a class! And when we're there, there's a real sense of community, but also a bit of healthy competition, which drives greater levels of performance. There's a common feature in most CrossFit boxes (gyms): the PR bell. It's literally a bell that you ring when you're achieved a personal record in weightlifting or gymnastics, etc. Celebrating the small wins in a community is a powerful motivator.

Take action

- Write a list of your daily habits and assess which ones are supporting or hindering progress towards your goals.

- Breathe. Just taking a moment to focus on your breath is a powerful tool allowing you to return to the present moment and *respond* rather than react.

- Take small steps, like scheduling one minute of mindfulness a day, and build your mindfulness muscle over time.

- Create the right environment for your healthy habits. Make it easy to change.

- Find your tribe. Set yourself up for success by finding like-minded people who will support you on your journey.

8
A – Address Your Stress

We're obsessed with stress. Talk to anyone and they will say they're feeling stressed and over-stretched. The Covid pandemic has supercharged our stress, taking it to a new level. Bad news sells news-papers – 'if it bleeds, it leads' – and there's been no shortage of bad news. But how do we break out of this endless stress cycle, something we know is deeply damaging to our health and our performance?

Change your state

It may sound overly simplistic, but we just have to STOP. So, **S**top, **T**ake a deep breath, **O**bserve the situation objectively and then **P**roceed in a logical manner (as opposed to a reactive one). This little, but powerful, mindfulness practice was originally developed by Jon Kabatt-Zin, one of the leading minds in mindfulness and creator of the Mindfulness Based Stress Reduction Programme in the late 1970s.[59] It helps us to change our state in the moment from a sympathetic nervous state (fight or flight) to a parasympathetic one. From here, we start to feel more in control and can make better, more informed decisions. Let's unpack this exercise to see how to practically apply it:

- **Stop:** It can often be difficult to recognise when our stress boils over and we start reacting, as opposed to responding in a logical, well thought through manner. Sometimes, the situation is so critical that it may even seem impossible to take a break and change our state to a calmer, more measured one, but these are exactly the times when we need this practice the most. As discussed in Chapter Seven, practising mindfulness regularly, when you're not in crisis mode, will help build that muscle and make it easier to interrupt the stress pattern when things get to a critical level.

- **Take a breath:** Deep, calm breathing is the best way of telling the body that things are under control and it's OK to withdraw the troops. No need to fight or flee; we're in control of the situation.

- **Observe the situation:** Don't judge. Just observe. In his play, *Hamlet*, Shakespeare famously wrote, 'There is nothing either good or bad, but thinking makes it so.'[60] Recall our earlier discussion regarding perception being our reality. Facts are neither good nor bad: it's our interpretation of the facts that determines whether we become stressed and narrow our vision, or view the situation with a sense of perspective. Simply observing will allow us to consider all the options for addressing the challenge or problem we are facing.

- **Proceed:** Now that we have given ourselves some space to objectively consider all the options, we can proceed in an informed manner. This may include taking into consideration input from others.

It requires a lot of practice for STOP to become our default response. When we're faced with an angry boss or a customer screaming in our face, it can take everything we have to break that stress response pattern and give ourselves that little bit of space and time to compose ourselves and be able to respond in a rational way. Try literally calling for a time-out and, ideally, ask the other party involved to take a deep breath too!

Identify your stressors

Once we've changed our state by practising the STOP exercise, or any other form of mindfulness practice, we can then objectively assess what's causing the stress.

The likelihood is that it will be a combination of several factors (including some that you may not have even been conscious of), and when they all come together, it can be difficult to manage them. A useful exercise is to literally list everything that may be contributing to the stressful situation. Which of these issues do you have control over? For example, we generally don't have any control over things like the weather, morning traffic, volcanic eruptions, wars, or news in the media, so it will not help us in any way if we let them bother us. In some cases, we are not completely helpless.

One of the ways to manage stress from negative news is to limit our exposure to news in the media. If you are particularly concerned about a social issue, perhaps getting involved in a useful way will make you feel better about it. On the other hand, if something is totally out of our control, like the weather, worrying about it doesn't make any sense and is a waste of our energy and brain power. By identifying our stressors and dividing them into the three categories below, we can form a plan for dealing with the ones we have control, or partial control, over and ignore the rest. Having a plan puts us back in control, which is a less stressful position to be in.

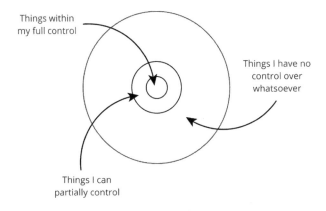

Things within
my full control

Things I have no
control over
whatsoever

Things I can
partially control

Stressor rings

As noted in Chapter Three, we actually can't live without some stress. When we are exposed to too much stress (ie chronic stress), it can be damaging to our health. At the same time, too little stress or challenge in our lives also has negative consequences. Through her research on the effect of stress on the brain, Yale Professor Amy Arnsten has shown that not having enough challenge or 'stress' leads to the brain producing less of the hormones associated with stress and can leave us feeling unmotivated and lethargic.[61] The right amount of stress and, therefore, the hormones that enable us to deal with challenges, is what she refers to as the 'Goldilocks' zone. By trying to stay within the Goldilocks zone, we can ensure that we have just the right amount of stress to keep us motivated and operating at our highest potential without burning ourselves out.

As a practical exercise, try to identify those areas in life where you feel challenged, but fulfilled. Those are examples of being in the Goldilocks zone: just enough of those stress hormones to keep you motivated, but not enough to push you into chronic stress. By incorporating these activities into your daily routine, practising the STOP method and identifying your stressors, you will start to notice the difference in your stress levels and your ability to manage stressful situations.

NATASA'S STORY

We recently had a 'perfect storm' of stressors when we were caught in the dramatic fall of the markets as a result of the war in Ukraine, the travel chaos at the tail end of Covid and the spike in oil prices. Added to this, we had a leak in our basement, some health issues with close family members and some significant, competing deadlines for our work. In the background, there was the constant barrage of bad news in the media. It was only after listing everything that was contributing to our stressful situation that we were able to pick our different stressors apart and recognise that there were a number of things that we had control over (such as our exposure to the media) or things that we had partial control over (getting in a professional to fix the leak). Then there were the things that we had no control over, such as the war and the collapse of the financial markets. But even in the case of the latter two, we could do things to help change our thoughts and feelings about them and, consequently, reduce the level of stress. To help deal with the devastating reality of the war, we volunteered to help Ukrainian families, including hosting one in our home. As for the disastrous performance of our investments, firstly (and most importantly), we looked for perspective to our guest family from Ukraine who had lost everything. Secondly, we had the possibility and the tools to restructure our investments to mitigate our exposure. Ultimately, things always resolve themselves one way or another.

Decompress

The other key to managing stress is to allow ourselves to decompress by having adequate time to recover after dealing with a stressful event. When we provide our bodies and minds adequate recovery from stress, we elevate our baseline for dealing with a similar level of stress in the future. It's like building muscle or increasing our endurance levels when we exercise. The process of building muscle or increasing endurance occurs *after* the workout, when the body repairs the 'damage' created during the workout. When we don't give ourselves adequate recovery time after a workout, we can do more harm than good. This is what leads to injury in the long-term. Similarly, giving ourselves adequate recovery time after a stressful event builds resilience to future stressful events. Inadequate recovery time can lead to chronic stress and burnout.

An interesting line of research in the area of stress management is the concept of the ultradian rhythm. You will recall that our circadian rhythm is about 24 hours and controls our sleep-wake cycles. Our ultradian rhythm is made up of roughly ninety-minute cycles in the day, during which our productivity levels experience peaks and troughs. According to performance psychologists, Jim Loehr and Tony Schwartz,

> 'Physiological measures such as heart rate, hormonal levels, muscle tension and brain-wave activity all increase during the first part of the cycle – and so does alertness. After an hour or so, these measures start to decline. Somewhere between 90 and 120 minutes, the body begins to crave a period of rest and recovery.'[62]

By understanding and working with these cycles, we can maximise our performance during the day and avoid burning out.

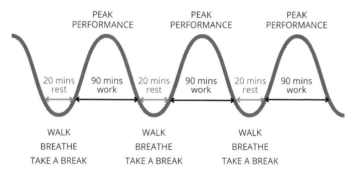

Ultradian rhythm

Maintaining a healthy balance in each of the other drivers – nutrition, movement and sleep – are essential for recovery in general, but also to recover from stressful events. For example, a balanced diet not only supports a healthy immune system, but it also provides the extra energy needed to cope with stressful events. Physical activity helps to lower blood pressure and stress hormone levels. Low to moderate exercise, like walking or cycling, increases breathing and heart rate so that more oxygen reaches cells throughout the body. It also reduces tension in our muscles, including the heart.[63] Sleep is the great soother. As we will discover in Chapter Twelve, there is actually a mechanism for soothing over the stressors that have occurred during the day. The irony is that when we're stressed, it becomes more difficult to get to, and stay, asleep. The secret to managing stress and getting a good night's sleep is as simple as it is profound: just breathe!

We tend to take breathing for granted. It is, after all, something what we don't even need to think about. It happens automatically. Breathing is one of those functions (like the beating of our heart) that is controlled by our autonomic nervous system. Our breathing patterns change in response to a threat (fight or flight) or if we are resting or digesting. However, we can actually take control of our breathing at any time and use it to change our state. We personally use three simple breathing exercises regularly to re-energise, rebalance and relax:

1. **Energising breathing** is to be used sparingly if you need a boost of energy, for example, in the morning (instead of coffee) or before exercise. Be careful not to overuse it. Like coffee, it has its place and role and overusing it can cause anxiety. Those of you who are familiar with *pranayama* might know this breathing technique as 'the breath of fire'. You basically only focus on pushing sharp, short exhales from your abdomen and allowing your inhale to happen automatically. It feels a bit as if you are sneezing. Ten repetitions should be enough.

2. **Balancing breathing** is good for you any time. This breathing will be beneficial to you any time of the day whenever you feel the need to rebalance and recentre. Sit down, put your hands on your lap, relax your shoulders and close your eyes. Breathing in and out through your nose, inhale to a count of four and then exhale to a count of four. Repeat ten times.

3. **Relaxing breathing** is amazing for relaxation and is primarily to be used to fall asleep without pills or alcohol. Lay down on your back. Put your right hand on your chest and your left hand on your belly. Your right hand should remain still and your left hand should rise and fall with your breath as you practise. Close your eyes. Breathing in and out through your nose, inhale to the count of four and then exhale to the count of eight. Repeat ten times or until you fall asleep.

Using your breath mindfully and purposefully not only helps to switch between your sympathetic and parasympathetic nervous systems, but also to become more present and to turn off your autopilot.

Take action

- STOP stressing about stress. Literally: Stop, Take a deep breath, Observe the situation objectively and, only then, Proceed.

- Identify your stressors. Make a plan of sensible actions to address those stressors within or partially within your control, and let go of those you have no influence over.

- Reframe your mindset. See if you can view stress as an opportunity for growth and learning.

- Work with your natural rhythms (both circadian and ultradian). Take a break every 90 minutes during the day and be consistent with your sleep routine.

- We can't stress (pun intended) enough: just breathe! Breathing is the most effective way to instantly change your state and deal with stress.

9
K – Know Your 'Why'

We've all experienced the frustration of keeping our new year's resolutions. The end of a year is a good time to reflect on our lives, and we often realise that there are things we really should change. Health issues often top the list, and we feel so committed to begin with: 'This time it will be different. This time I'll really lose those extra kilos (which have, incidentally, increased even more over the past year). I'll start using that gym membership I signed up to two years ago and have used a total of three times.' Sound familiar?

Finding your purpose

Why is it that we can't translate our good intentions into lasting action? For one thing, most resolutions rely almost entirely on willpower, and while willpower is critical to get us going initially, it tends to fail us when we need it the most and is not enough to make sustainable changes. Even when we have all the necessary information supporting our decision to change, we don't necessarily act accordingly. We do need to have the facts – the 'How' and the 'What' – but, ultimately, we make decisions based on our emotions: the 'Why'. In his book *Start with Why: How great leaders inspire everyone to take action*, Simon Sinek explains that we need to start with the 'Why' to make real, sustainable change.[64] He is talking about the application of the idea at a corporate level, but the principle also applies to individuals.

Our brain's ultimate job is to keep us safe and alive. Its attitude is, 'If it ain't broke, don't change it.' As long as you have a pulse, your brain will do everything to keep you operating in ways that are familiar – even if, ultimately, they turn out to be bad for you. To paraphrase Grug from *The Croods*, 'Change is bad. Change gets you killed.'[65] But that crude (pardon the pun), ancient side of our brain can ultimately be overridden by appealing to an equally powerful urge to fulfil our true purpose. As a species, we are capable of amazing feats when we are rooted in a purpose so deep that it becomes almost an obsession. Our purpose, or Why, can be a powerful source of motivation and drive, even in the most difficult circumstances. It's what gets us out of bed on a cold, wet Monday morning to go for that jog because we know that one small act takes us closer to our ultimate goal, to fulfilling our purpose.

JIM'S STORY

Turning fifty was a real milestone for me. Call it a midlife crisis, but I had a strong sense that if I was going to live another fifty years (fingers crossed, maybe even more), I needed to make some serious changes. But why would this be any different than other, countless times where I had tried various 'fixes' but, ultimately, nothing had worked? Well, a big part of my failure was that I wasn't entirely sure of why I was trying to change. Of course, there were the basic, low-level concerns like, 'I hate the way I look in the mirror and probably should shed a few pounds/kilos,' or, 'I'm tired of feeling tired all of the time.' Without a real sense of *why* I wanted to change, it was difficult to implement, and stick to, any kind of regime. And when things got difficult, like being busy or stressed at work or home, it was so easy to fall off the wagon just long enough to go back to square one and have to start the cycle all over again – a scenario that was deeply demotivating and which made it hard to even contemplate restarting.

Natasa's frustration levels with her own health were similar and we often talked about what steps we could, and should, take in order to change. At that time, Natasa was helping businesses solve human-centric challenges with a positive psychology framework called AI (Appreciative Inquiry).[66] Suddenly, a lightbulb went off in our heads: why couldn't we use the same approach to solve *our* health issues? So, that's what we did. We followed the four stages of the framework:

- We started by rediscovering our values – things that we valued and appreciated the most – as well as what we really enjoyed doing.

127

- We imagined our most desired future broken down into different areas of life.
- We looked at the processes, resources and relationships that would take us to that ideal future.
- We made an action plan.

This simple, but extremely efficient, process helped both of us gain clarity on our Why by getting us beyond all of the usual superficial reasons. I now knew why it was so important for me to be in peak health and performance: to develop and protect my physical body and maintain my physical health and wellbeing into old age. I clearly saw myself as a great father and husband, who was more present and had the vitality to keep up with five growing boys and a beautiful, active wife. I also had a clear picture on the process, resources and relationships to get me to my ultimate goal, as well as an initial action plan.

Natasa's deepest Why was to break free from limiting beliefs about her physical body and to become the best version of herself – with more energy, creativity and focus. To be the best mother, wife and human being possible. Any time we need reminding of why we're doing this, we simply refer back to our individual Why.

Going through the exercise of putting your health into perspective with your greater purpose or vision and anchoring it to a deeply meaningful reason is very powerful. How does a healthy life serve your grand goals? What's your real motivation for wanting to change? For example, having a goal of losing

10 kilos for a friend's wedding is a short-term goal that is probably feasible. You can go on a crash diet, maybe pound yourself with cardio for a couple of months and show up at the wedding fitting in your suit/dress. A word of caution, though. There's a strong likelihood that you will rebound with the weight, and maybe even gain a bit more. However, if your purpose is to improve your overall health because you want to be the best version of yourself and perform at your highest level, both at work and in your private life, now we're starting to get somewhere. Dig deeper, find something that really resonates with your core values and your purpose, and then harness that passion to ignite your motivation.

Follow your strategy

Once you're crystal clear on your Why, it's important to have a strategy to get there. A vision on its own doesn't get you anywhere. Identifying the action you need to take in the short-, medium- and long-term will provide you with way-markers for the journey. The more specific and detailed the steps are, the more likely you are to follow the plan. The AI process and framework referred to above will also help you to map out a firm strategy or action plan for achieving your goals.

NATASA'S STORY

One of my biggest shortcomings when it came to staying healthy was having a clear strategy and sticking with it. I often found myself doing things that seemed sensible at the time, but were ultimately counterproductive and did not contribute to my long-term vision. For example, when I was younger, I used to do a lot of cardio to maintain a good body composition. My diet wasn't horrible, but it seemed like I could 'get away' with some unhealthy eating if I occasionally went on crash diets and visited the gym a bit more. Unfortunately, in the short-term, I did some serious damage to my knees and hips doing excessive step aerobics, which were all the rage in the nineties (now I've just given away my age!). In the longer term, going on trendy diets did more harm than good and made it more difficult to keep the weight off.

When I finally got serious about having longer-term goals linked to my Why and came up with a concrete strategy with a clearly defined action plan, the process became more straightforward and I started to see real results. Recognising the interaction between mindset (having my Why), nutrition (eating sensibly for my stage of life and level of activity), a balanced exercise plan, and good sleep (giving my body the chance to recover and rejuvenate) was a game-changer.

A powerful exercise to formalise your Why and commit to your strategy is to sign a Personal Health Contract with yourself. Set out your Why in detail and then lay out your step-by-step strategy for achieving it.

You're now formally committed to achieving your health goals and can start to execute your strategy.

Check in from time to time

Your Why and your strategy for achieving your goals are based on your core values and your deepest desires to make the necessary changes, so they should remain pretty constant, but it's good practice to check in from time to time to make sure you're still on the right path. It may be that the strategy needs tweaking to help you to achieve your ultimate goal. Our lives are constantly changing and sometimes circumstances intervene and can have a material impact on our journey to health, for example, starting a new job, getting married or divorced, having children or becoming empty-nesters. All of these are major events that may trigger a rethink of your motivation and strategy.

As you learn and grow, you can incorporate your new lessons and experiences into your Why as a kind of 'addendum' to your Personal Health Contract. It is *absolutely vital* not to beat yourself up when life intervenes and you occasionally 'deviate from the flight plan'. As humans, we are hardwired to focus on the negatives. Focus on what you can control and do your best in the current circumstances. Also realise that the sooner you can course correct, the easier it is to get back on track. We can easily slip back into old, unhealthy habits if we spend too much time off course.

Take action

- Become super clear on your Why. Your deepest Why that aligns with your values will keep you motivated to change your habits for a healthier life.

- Align your health goals with your grand life goals.

- Have a strategy. Be super specific, commit to it and sign your Personal Health Contract to make it even more real.

- Check in regularly to make sure you're still on track. Make course corrections if necessary.

- Celebrate any successes along the way to stay motivated, learn from mistakes and fall forwards.

10

E – Eat Yourself Healthy

At a time when the majority of the Western world is overfed and undernourished, knowing what food is actually nourishing for us is of critical importance. Good quality food is vital for our health and optimal performance. Besides physical nourishment, a healthy meal prepared and shared with friends and family is a powerful emotional booster and a way to bond, destress and replenish your oxytocin and endorphin levels. Our bodies, minds and souls depend on the fuel that we put in them for health, clarity of thoughts, energy and general wellbeing.

Nourishment

Our nourishment comes from macronutrients (water, fibre, proteins, carbohydrates and fats) and micronutrients (vitamins and minerals). Both of the nutrient categories are important and to thrive, we need a good balance and diversity of both.

Carbohydrates provide short-term energy, fats are a long-term fuel and proteins are our building blocks. We are, quite literally, what we eat. Water is absolutely indispensable, as the human body is made up of about 60% water.[67] Fibre is the main source of nourishment for our gut bacteria, which support our brain, heart, immune system and metabolic health. Vitamins are organic matter, while minerals are inorganic compounds (found in soil, water and rocks) that we ingest through plant and animal products.

You might be tempted to look for a perfect combination of these components for optimal health and performance, but there is no such thing. We each have a unique body, we are at different stages of life, live in different climates and have different health and performance goals. The crucial points to remember are to listen to the signals your body sends, eat the natural human diet (used in the correct sense of the word) and fast periodically. This will help you thrive regardless of your age and food preferences. Let's dive in.

Eat mindfully

You have already learned that mindfulness (aka mental presence) is a superpower when you want to turn off autopilot or to manage stress. Interestingly, it is also incredibly powerful in the case of eating.

The lost connection

Mindful eating engages our parasympathetic nervous system (rest and digest) and shifts our attention to the connection between our food, our body and our brain.[68] At a time when most of us eat while doing something else (answering emails, reading, watching Netflix, etc), this connection has been completely lost and we can no longer interpret the signals our body is constantly sending us. For example, have you ever ignored a headache? Here is an interesting fact. One of the most common causes of headaches is dehydration. So, before you pop a painkiller while you're on autopilot, stop for a minute and think. Maybe all you need is to drink some water.

Another example is a common favourite: pizza. How do you feel about eating pizza? You've probably already started salivating just thinking about this delicious food. But, how do you feel *after* having a pizza? The reactions might be a bit more varied to this question, but most of us ideally like a couch to be close by to take a nap afterwards. We feel heavy and sleepy, and some of us may experience pain or an upset stomach. At night, we may toss and turn and wake up cranky and bloated. That's our bodies talking to us! Now, we're not saying never to have pizza again (especially if you are in Italy), but do pay attention to how your body reacts to food. And remember, the way your body reacts is unique to you.

Our internal dialogue

For most people, this is a difficult concept. Nobody wants to seem crazy. 'What do you mean, I have voices in my head?' We all do, but we often choose to just ignore them. Once we start to listen to our internal dialogue, it gives us a lot of insight into how we operate. With understanding and self-compassion, this helps us to then change our potentially destructive eating habits into healthy ones.

Have you ever debated with yourself about having 'just one more, small slice of chocolate cake'? Or found yourself standing in front of the fridge looking for 'something'? No? Are you sure? Next time it happens, STOP. Yes, we mean use the STOP method described in Chapter 8: stop, take a deep breath and observe what's happening. Are you really hungry, is it mealtime or are you actually trying to change a certain state (eg boredom, loneliness or feeling overwhelmed)? Once you have established the underlying thought or emotion, you are ready to make a *conscious* decision and proceed with intention. You may choose to eat, or you may do something else that will help you change your state, such as walk your dog, hug your partner or do a 5-minute breathing practice.

Another valuable exercise is to list the food rules that you set for yourself. These rules may be something like: 'My life is too stressful to give up coffee and wine,'[69] 'A birthday without a cake is not a real celebration,' 'Friday is pizza night,' or, 'I deserve a treat for making it through another week.' What are your rules? Are they serving you well?

Digestion starts in the brain

Even before we taste food, our brain registers and sends signals to our digestive system to start preparing for what's coming. In other words, the brain lets the gut know that it's time to rev up, produce the necessary enzymes and get ready to digest incoming food. When we eat while multitasking, we are skipping this first part of the digestion process, which impedes the proper absorption of nutrients. Multitasking also increases stress, which activates the fight or flight response. This tells the gut to shut down and so food is not digested properly. Equally important, eating while distracted not only results in overeating at that particular meal, but it also might make you eat more later on.[70] So, to appreciate your food and properly digest it, it is important to tune in and be present for the joyous experience of eating.

NATASA'S STORY

My brother and I live in different countries. We are very close, but we don't manage to speak very often, as we both have busy lives. When he does call, I usually prioritise him over anything else I am doing. It happened that he once called while I was getting ready to eat lunch. I decided I would talk to him anyway, while eating. We had a great chat: I finished lunch and even got ready to leave for a meeting in town while we were talking. As I arrived in the city, I felt a strong desire to eat. I couldn't have been hungry, because I had just eaten 30 minutes ago, but it felt as though I'd missed out on a meal. My brain did not register that I'd had a nutritious meal because it was busy with the conversation with my brother! Luckily, I was *aware* of what was going on and it saved me from grabbing something on the go. Instead, I just had some water. My awareness helped me not to overeat and, as a bonus, to stay hydrated.

Last but not least, remember to thoroughly chew your food. Chewing increases the surface area of the food. This helps the stomach to digest and, consequently, your small intestine to better absorb, the nutrients.

Eat natural foods

Eat real food

To know what real food is, ask yourself: 'Did nature make it, or is it man-made (ie processed food)?' If you can grow it, hunt it or catch it, then eat it. Otherwise, try and stay away from it. If you do opt for packaged food, read the label carefully. There should not be more than five ingredients, and you should be able to recognise all of them. A good rule of thumb: if your grandmother would recognise the ingredients, you can eat it.

Eat wholesome, unprocessed food. Importantly, white flour, white sugar and white rice are processed, meaning they have been stripped of the majority of their nutrients. Eat as much organic food as possible. Good quality produce, meat and fish mean that your body will ingest the maximum amount of nutrients with a minimum (or hopefully none) of the nasty toxins.

Eat food in season

Fruit and vegetables (ideally locally sourced) are fresher, more nutritious and tastier when harvested in season. And while chicken, pork and beef are available all year round, we should not forget that our meat can also be seasonal. Autumn is abundant in a variety of game such as pheasant, duck, wild boar, venison and rabbit, to mention just a few of our favourites.

For many of us, it may be difficult to know what's in season, as most of the vegetables and fruits are now available all year round due to farming practices and global transportation. A good strategy is to go to the local farmer's market and talk to the producers themselves. Living in the Netherlands, our experience is that these markets will still sell bananas (clearly never in season locally) but, for the most part, there will be an abundance of local, seasonal vegetables and fruit that are natural, fresh and absolutely delicious. We also really enjoy interacting with the people who actually grow the food and are passionate about it.

If you live in a big city and getting to a farmers' market is not an option, we recommend googling what's in season in your local area and then shopping for local produce, even if it's just at your supermarket. You will most certainly eat healthier, save some money and, potentially, our planet.

It's important to remember that our bodies evolved to thrive on seasonal variations of produce. Even if you can't, or don't, want to follow natural seasons, you should still follow the principle of seasonality: don't eat the same fruits and vegetables all year round. It is also advisable to take a break from fruit in general for a few weeks now and then, due to its high sugar content.

Eat the rainbow

All fruits and vegetables contain vitamins, minerals and so-called phytochemicals that are essential to fight oxidative stress, enhance the immune system, support heart and brain health, reduce inflammation and promote our health in general. Oxidative stress is an imbalance of free radicals and antioxidants in the body that plays a big role in ageing. Research suggests that long-term oxidative stress contributes to the development of a large range of chronic conditions, such as cancer, heart disease and diabetes.[71] An interesting fact is that the colour and the smell of the plants are largely determined by these phytochemicals. The bigger the variety, the better for your health. You may have noticed that a lot of mass-produced fruit and vegetables, or those produced outside of their natural season, just don't taste and smell the same as their naturally, seasonally grown equivalents. This is because they don't have the same levels of vitamins, minerals and phytochemicals.

Nutrients grouped by food colour

	Main nutrients	What to eat	Best for
Red	Lycopene, anthocyanin	Tomatoes, watermelon, strawberries, red peppers, cherries, raspberries, beets	Heart health and cancer risk reduction (prostate, breast, and lung)
Orange	Vitamin C, beta-carotene, folate	Carrots, sweet potatoes, cantaloupe, mangoes, apricots, oranges	Immune system, skin health, wound healing, heart health and cancer risk reduction
Yellow	Lycopene, beta-carotene	Squash, yellow peppers, pineapples, lemons, grapefruits	Eye health, digestion, immune system

(Continued)

Nutrients grouped by food colour (*cont.*)

	Main nutrients	What to eat	Best for
Green	Chlorophyll, lutein, fibre, vitamins K and B	Broccoli, spinach, dark leafy greens, avocados, peas, asparagus, kiwifruit	Energy, digestion, lung health and detoxification, cancer risk reduction
Blue	Anthocyanins, resveratrol, flavonoids, folate	Blueberries, blackberries, eggplants, blackcurrants, plums, red cabbage, red onions	Brain health, risk reduction of age-related cognitive decline and neurodegenerative diseases
White	Potassium, allium compounds, polyphenols, folate	Mushrooms, potatoes, onions, garlic, turnips, parsnips	Heart health and cancer risk reduction (colon, stomach and prostate)

Fasting

You probably find yourself in situations where the food options are not the healthiest, or the timing for eating is not ideal. That's life. In this part of the book, we hope to strengthen your confidence that not only is it absolutely safe to skip a meal (or two, or even three), but doing so is actually good, and even necessary, for your physical and mental health. So, next time you know you won't have a chance to properly nourish yourself, grab your water bottle and plan for a fast.

As we discussed in Chapter Four, we have evolved to go for long periods of time without food. This ingenious evolutionary adaptation to different levels of food availability due to climate conditions, the seasons and the fluctuation of our own energy expenditure has made us metabolically flexible by design. For 99.5% of human history, food availability was highly unreliable.[72] Now, in the Western world, we are living in an unprecedented time of food abundance and there is an unprecedented number of people with metabolic disorders and related diseases.

The significant benefits of fasting have been known for millennia. Throughout history, fasting has been used as a powerful healing therapy, but we have largely forgotten about it for some time. It is only in the past couple of decades that health experts and researchers have started to discuss it again and promote it as part of healthy living.

Earlier, we described gut health, metabolic flexibility and hormone health as the three key areas of focus of nutrition science. It will not surprise you that all three significantly benefit from fasting. Fasting boosts the microbiome,[73] balances blood sugar, improves insulin sensitivity, improves metabolic health, enhances cognitive performance, decreases the risk of heart diseases and obesity and supports longevity. One interesting, additional benefit is that fasting, like exercise, is a form of hormetic (healthy) stress and, as such, promotes resilience over time.

One of the biggest concerns people have about fasting is that they will feel hungry so let's talk about the types of hunger you may experience during fasting:

Thirst

Thirst is a type of hunger? This might sound counterintuitive, but there is a possible, and an evolutionarily plausible, reason. In our cave-dwelling days, we did not have water bottles to carry around with us, but we needed to stay hydrated. If we were lucky, we were close to a body of water, but that was not always the case. Thankfully, much of the food available to us contained a lot of water. Think about the fresh plants, fruits and tubers. So, when the body felt it was time to rehydrate, it sent a signal to the brain to eat! Hardly accidentally, the same part of our brain is responsible for interpreting both hunger and thirst signals.

There is a lot of controversy about how much water you really need, but as we mentioned, about 60% of the human adult body is made up of water. The brain and heart are composed of 73% water and the lungs are about 83% water. The skin contains 64% water and our muscles and kidneys contain 79%. Even our bones are watery, with a 31% water content.[74]

The problem with our modern lifestyle is that it is highly dehydrating. Think coffee, alcohol and processed food that's full of salt and sugar, all of which *remove* water from our system. So, be aware of the importance of hydration and don't just pop open another bag of crisps when you feel hungry. Depending on your body size and the climate you live in, you need about two to three litres of water a day. So, drink up.

Emotional hunger

Food is such a powerful soother that often we use it to deal with our emotional 'hunger'. Some of us reach for a chocolate when, in reality, we need a hug. Others graze on nuts all day because they are bored. Yet others might empty the fridge at night after a stressful day at work. As we mentioned earlier, the STOP technique is very useful in these cases. Are you really hungry, or is there an emotion that you are seeking to change? You might be surprised how often we use food to manage our emotional discomfort or pain.

Empty stomach hunger

You might think, 'Here it is. Real hunger!' In a way, it is. Your stomach will empty every 3-4 hours and then you might experience that 'empty stomach feeling'. But if you have ever gone without food for a prolonged period of time, you will know that you don't simply become hungrier and hungrier as time passes. On the contrary, after about 48 hours, you don't feel hungry at all. But, let's not go that far just yet. Your hunger pangs will only last for about 20 minutes at a time, and then they will go away. In the meantime, there are effective ways to take your mind off your hunger: drink some water, go for a walk, do a breathing exercise or call a friend. Or do Natasa's favourite: just get busy! Take advantage of the additional energy and focus that fasting brings.

Types of fasts

Fasts can vary in length, as well as what's 'allowed' during fasting, depending on your experience level and your goal.

Intermittent fasting allows you a window of a certain number of hours during which can eat, and you then fast the rest of the time. One of the most popular schedules is the 16:8 plan. This is where you fast for 16 hours and eat during a window of 8 hours. It could look something like this: finish dinner at 8:30pm, skip breakfast, and have lunch at 12:30pm. Or, finish a late lunch at 3pm, skip dinner and have breakfast at 7am.

Other popular regimens are 14:10, 18:6, 20:4, and the so-called 'one meal a day' (OMAD), where you have a window of one hour during which to eat. OMAD suits many of those with busy schedules. A big advantage of this plan is that you don't even have to think about what to eat or what to cook for the other two meals (or any snacks), so it frees up mental space and saves time. Talk about high efficiency. Depending on your health goals, alternate day eating or extended (36 hours-plus) fasts might also be beneficial. Here are a few tips for those new to fasting:

- The night is your friend, as you already fast for 7-8 hours when you sleep.

- Start with consistently fasting for 12 hours.

- Extend by one hour at a time by moving your dinner earlier and / or pushing your breakfast to later.

- Eat a small, low-carb meal before you start your fast.

- Break your fast gently with a small portion of cooked vegetables or a small egg dish with avocado.

- Stay well hydrated and keep a bottle of water with you at all times.

In terms of what you can consume, there are also a number of options. A water fast is called a 'clean' fast. In this case, you only drink water and make sure that you stay well hydrated. Other fasts allow you to drink tea, coffee (black, with cream or MCT oil[75]) or bone broth. All of these are good options that allow you to feel more comfortable during your fast while still enjoying significant benefits.

The fasting process

What's happening in your body when you fast?

- **4–8 hours:** All food has left the stomach, our blood sugar returns to base level, and insulin is no longer produced.

- **12 hours:** The digestion process is finished and our body can start repairing and healing itself. The production of the human growth hormone (HGH) increases, which boosts cell reproduction and regeneration.

- **14 hours:** Our body starts using our own fat for energy.

- **18 hours:** Fat burning increases and autophagy starts.[76]

- **24 hours:** Fat burning and autophagy ramp up. As glucose stores become depleted, ketones are released into our bloodstream for fuel.

- **36 hours:** Autophagy increases dramatically and the body continues to burn its own fat. This is a great fast for weight loss.

- **48 hours:** Autophagy increases even further, our immune system resets, and our inflammatory response reduces. We tend to feel no, or very little, hunger.

- **72 hours:** Autophagy maxes out and ketone production increases and becomes the primary fuel for the brain.

For most of us, fasting will result in immense health benefits and help balance the negative environmental impact of our modern sedentary and convenience-focused lives. The key is to build a fasting lifestyle that suits *your* life and to be consistent.

A word of caution: Fasting is not a panacea for all health issues and is not necessarily good for everyone. For one, women and men should fast differently, because of the hormonal differences (please check out the Recommended Reading section at the end of the book for some resources). Fasting is not recommended for children, pregnant women, those who would like to get pregnant or those who are breastfeeding. If you have a medical condition, it is best to consult your doctor before considering any long fast.

Take action

- Start noticing your eating patterns and write them down. You might be confusing thirst or an emotion that you're dealing with for hunger.

- Clean up your fridge and pantry. Get rid of all the processed stuff and fill them up with real food.

- Get to know what's in season where you live and buy from local sources.

- Get into the routine of drinking water. Get yourself a cool-looking (BPA-free) water bottle and keep it with you. Whenever in doubt, just drink.

- Stop multitasking while eating, as it literally impedes digestion. Instead, eat mindfully – enjoy your food.

- Fast for at least 13 hours a day (overnight). Give your body the chance to do all the amazing repair work it needs to do.

11

O – Overhaul Your Movement

In Part Two, we established that there is an evolutionary imperative for us to move. Movement is not only necessary for our physical and mental health, but also for our overall performance in life. We shouldn't think of this as a 'bad' thing or something we 'have to do'. Instead, we should consider it as giving a gift to our bodies which improves our health and performance in return. When we change our mindset around movement from being something that only athletes need to do, to something critical to our health and performance, then everything changes. We become passionate about moving and find all sorts of ways to increase our amount and variety of movement.

NATASA'S STORY

Jim and I have completely changed our perspective on movement. Jim used to think that going to the gym was a pain, but something he had to do. I, on the other hand, didn't mind going to the gym, but I absolutely hated stairs (so much so that my dream has always been to live in a bungalow so I didn't have to deal with them). Fast forward a couple of years and Jim is now passionate about working out in the gym and we actually compete on how many flights of stairs we achieve during the day. Once we changed our mindsets around movement (including understanding it better from a health perspective), it completely transformed how we approach it in our day-to-day lives.

Just move

In Chapter Five, we were introduced to the WHO standards on the minimum amount of movement we need to be healthy. But how can we achieve these standards, and even exceed them to maximise our health and performance? The key is to find a balance between our ordinary, everyday movement (our NEAT) and how much physical exercise we then need to fill the gap.

A NEAT concept

NEAT refers to 'non-exercise activity thermogenesis'.[77] It's a bit of a mouthful, but in simple terms, NEAT is a measurement of how much energy you burn during the day before doing any physical exercise. For example, during a day where you go about your daily routine and do no physical exercise or workouts and you burn, say, 1,500 calories, this would be your baseline NEAT. If you're not particularly active in terms of your lifestyle, then you're probably not getting enough movement from your activity and would need to either increase your NEAT activity or supplement it with physical exercise. Before getting to physical exercise, let's look at some practical ways of increasing our NEAT:

- **Increase physical movement:** As discussed, we have managed to engineer a lot of the need for movement out of our lives. Walking or biking instead of taking the car everywhere can dramatically increase our NEAT. Walking is an amazing physical activity that is gentle on our joints and greatly improves blood and oxygen circulation. Similarly, taking the stairs instead of elevators and escalators has a powerful impact on overall health, including improved metabolism and heart health.[78]

- **Up the intensity:** In addition to increasing normal daily physical movement, we can dramatically increase the intensity and, therefore, effectiveness and efficiency of our movement. For example, we can increase our heart rate by walking more vigorously. By breathing more deeply, we also increase our blood oxygen levels.

- **Play!** If you have kids or grandkids, the most rewarding form of NEAT is playing with them. Have you ever noticed that kids rarely just walk anywhere? They're usually running, jumping or skipping around. Try keeping up with a five- or six-year-old and you'll see what I mean. Also, if your child likes to be carried, it's a great weighted workout for you, increasing your strength and improving your heart health. No kids? Find a fun sport to play. Team sports are great for building strength and cardio capacity and are also fun, stress-relieving activities.

JIM'S STORY

Natasa and I have really worked on increasing our NEAT and being intentional about our ordinary movements. As an example, when we go into town, we either ride our bikes or, if we need to bring the car, we park it on level −3 in the underground car park. We always take the same spot – the one that's furthest from the stairs. This means we have an additional 300 metres or so (round trip) to get to and from the stairs, and then six flights of stairs to navigate. If we have groceries to carry back to the car, this can increase our NEAT considerably.

Below is a real-life example of us measuring NEAT versus physical exercise. What's really interesting is that in the weekend example, Jim achieved a higher number of 'active' zone minutes without having done any actual exercise. Just by doing weekend activities such as playing with our son, cleaning out the goats' pen and doing some vigorous gardening, he achieved more results than on a weekday when he would normally do a pretty vigorous workout. The power of NEAT!

The power of NEAT

	Activity	Zone minutes
Weekdays	NEAT: general daily movement	10
	3 x 10 minutes walking	30
	30 minutes of strength and conditioning workout	22
	TOTAL	62
Weekend	NEAT: bike ride, playing with our son, cleaning out the goats, gardening	35
	3 x 10 minutes of walking	30
	No workout	0
	TOTAL	65

Be more intentional

This refers to being mindful about your movement. For example, when you walk, start paying attention to what's going on in your body. Feel the exertion of your muscles and appreciate the health benefits you're providing your body. Breathe through your nose instead of your mouth. During nasal breathing, your nose releases nitric oxide, which improves oxygen circulation in your body.[79] Focusing on your breath also makes the activity more relaxing and it becomes an effective form of stress management. Walking in a green environment is like winning the mindfulness Trifecta: you also incorporate the benefits of 'forest bathing' (or 'green bathing'), which include improved immune response, better heart health, improved energy and sleep, enhanced mood, decreased inflammation and relief from joint pain.[80]

In an interesting study involving New York hotel cleaning staff, half of a group of eighty-four room attendants from seven different hotels were given an explanation of how the type of work they were performing was actually a highly effective physical activity regime. The other group were given no such explanation. When retested for the same health markers after four weeks, the tested group showed a decrease in weight, blood pressure, body fat, waist to hip ratio (WHR) and body mass index (BMI) compared to the control group, who experienced no such changes. The test group did not change their amount of activity during the four weeks and the physical changes they experienced appear to have been based solely on the fact that they were more aware of, and perhaps became more intentional about, the work they were doing.[81]

Mix it up

As previously discussed, in terms of our evolutionary design, our bodies have adapted and, indeed, require three main movement types: cardio, strength and mobility.

Cardio

Cardio includes any activity that gets the heart rate up, including walking, running, cycling, swimming, etc. There are two types of cardio activities: aerobic and anaerobic. These distinctions are important for determining what kind of activity may be appropriate for someone, depending on their fitness and health needs. Walking is an example of aerobic cardio in that the heart rate generally remains in the zone where the body can metabolise fat without having to resort to glycogen (sugar) stores in the muscles. It is an excellent activity for people who want to lose weight, as it speeds up the fat burning process. Anaerobic cardio involves elevating the heart rate to the point where there is not enough oxygen reaching the muscles and our metabolism switches to burning sugar. Anaerobic cardio exercises are good for heart health and increase our cardio capacity and stamina. Examples of anaerobic cardio are sprinting, weightlifting, rope jumping and sports that require constant movement, like tennis, basketball and football.

Strength

Strength or 'resistance' training involves physical activity that is designed to improve muscular fitness by exercising a muscle, or muscle group, against external resistance. Essentially, it involves lifting weights or other heavy objects, or using your own body weight to generate the resistance (callisthenics). As noted in Chapter Five, muscle strength is essential to our overall health and ability to function physically – especially as we age. A fundamental mistake many people make as they age is to give up any kind of strength training, as they associate it with an increased risk of injury. Ironically, many injuries as we age, including bone fractures from falling, are the result of a lack of strength training.[82]

Mobility and flexibility

Mobility and flexibility are sometimes used interchangeably, but they are slightly different. Flexibility involves the ability of a joint, or series of joints, to move through an unrestricted, pain-free range of motion. Having good mobility, on the other hand, enables someone to perform functional movements such as squats through the full range of motion. In other words, someone may be flexible (ie be able to achieve the full range of motion) but may not have the muscles or core strength to perform a movement with stability (ie they don't have enough mobility).

Why is it necessary to combine these types of movement to be physically healthy? Going back to our evolutionary origins, the movements we were doing back then were highly functional and involved elements of cardio, strength and mobility. We could not survive with just one or two. For example, what would be the benefit of being a fast runner to hunt an animal if we weren't strong enough to carry it back home? Like a three-legged stool, if one leg is missing, or one is weaker than the others, it destabilises the stool. Many people only focus on one or two of these movement types and this can cause health problems and imbalances. For example, people who focus primarily on strength training (eg bodybuilders) will generally have poor mobility and flexibility. Similarly, people who only run all the time will have good cardio endurance but often have lower muscle mass and strength, and may also lack overall mobility. Good health and fitness lie in the sweet spot between all three movement types.

Recover

Getting regular, varied movement back into our lives is crucial for our health and overall performance. Equally important is not to overdo it in terms of the intensity and volume of exercise. Exercise is a form of stress on our bodies that can become chronic and, therefore, counterproductive.[83] As explained above, our bodies adapt primarily in response to physical stress (eg lifting weight that is just beyond our comfort zone or getting our heart rate up beyond what we're normally used to). If we do this regularly, our bodies and brains get the idea that they need to adapt to handle this new 'normal'. Following these stressful events, the body goes about repairing any micro-damage done to the muscles or other related tissues. This process is referred to as 'recovery'. To allow the body to recover and, therefore, adapt to future stressors, we need to follow some basic principles:

Fuel your workout

As explained in Chapter Ten, we are what we eat. Nutrition provides the building blocks for every cell in our bodies. When we exercise vigorously (ie put our bodies under stress), we need all of the relevant building blocks to 'build back better'. If we're missing any of the required nutrients, then we can cause damage to our bodies. The key macros from a recovery perspective are carbohydrates to replace the stores of glycogen in your muscles that have been expended during the workout, and proteins and healthy fats to repair damage to the muscles and other tissues. Eating an overall balanced diet also provides the vitamins and minerals necessary for proper recovery.

Hydrate, hydrate, hydrate

A big part of recovery involves replacing hydration lost through sweat. Water also helps to remove the by-products of exercise, including lactate (the annoying stuff that causes that burning sensation in your muscles). If you're doing particularly intensive endurance exercise (eg running long distances), then add some salt or electrolytes such as potassium and sodium. These replace important minerals and can also prevent and relieve muscle cramping.

Allow for proper periods of recovery between reps and sets

Allowing the body these micro-periods of recovery means that the overall recovery time is reduced. For example, when lifting weights, pause for 60 to 90 seconds between reps or sets (or up to 3 minutes if the weight is particularly heavy).

Practise active recovery

Active recovery involves things like a cool down after the workout, such as stretching or going for a walk. You can also do some light exercise on rest days to keep the muscles active and improve blood circulation. This helps in preventing lactic acid buildup and to remove other toxins.

Sleep

As we'll discuss further in Chapter Twelve, sleep is the best form of recovery from physical and mental stress. Most of the repairs to our muscles happens during sleep. We produce human growth hormone (HGH) when we sleep. HGH helps to repair muscle tissue and build muscle mass after exercise. It also helps to boost metabolism and burn fat.

Other recovery tips

Many athletes use regular massage, sauna and/or cold-water therapy to assist in their recovery, but you don't need to be an athlete to take advantage of the benefits of these forms of recovery. Having a regular massage is a good idea for anyone as they boost our immunities, are a good way to detox – they speed up the exit of toxins from our bodies – and are a great way to destress. Hot and/or cold therapy may sound a bit extreme, but there is a lot of evidence that both (and also using them in combination) deliver a lot of health benefits, including improved recovery. Start with baby steps, like alternating between hot and cold in the shower. When you start to see the benefits, you can look into using saunas and cold plunging to maximise the benefits.[84]

Take action

- Do a NEAT audit to see where you can build more movement into your daily life.

- Find any excuse to move.

- Be mindful of your movement. Thinking about the movement while doing it makes it more efficient.

- Make a training plan. Include the activities that you already enjoy and add others to make sure you cover each movement type: cardio, strength and mobility.

- Treat your recovery with as much importance as your movement regime: fuel, hydrate and rest.

12

F – Fix Your Sleep

As with any changes we try to make, having the right mindset is half the battle. If we see sleep as an activity that benefits our health and performance, as opposed to something we can't avoid, then we are creating the right mindset to start building habits that will optimise our sleep. Hopefully, after our discussion in Part Two on sleep, you are amazed by its power to supercharge your health and performance. If you're not getting enough, you may be a bit terrified by the implications. You may also be frustrated by the fact that you realise the value of it but struggle to get enough good quality sleep. Either way, you are now ready to fix your sleep, so that you can take full advantage of its enormous health and performance benefits.

Sleep is also a great example of how the four health drivers work in unison. As we will see, the key to having a good night's sleep rests largely on optimising our mindset and our behaviours relating to nutrition and movement. Conversely, having good quality, and enough, sleep is critical for a healthy mindset and also supports good eating and movement habits. If you're tired, your motivation will be low, making it difficult to keep up with your movement and exercise. Your hormones will also be out of whack, making you hungry and setting off cravings for the wrong kinds of foods. This can lead to a downward spiral and derail your progress.

So, let's look at how we can maximise the quantity and quality of our sleep. An important point to consider is that, from a health and performance point of view, it is generally advised for adults to get a minimum of 7.5–8 hours of sleep.[85] That's a reference to the quantity of sleep we require. The other factor is the quality of that sleep. The discussion below deals with both factors, as achieving both is what really maximises the benefits of sleep. For example, we may spend 8 hours in bed, but if the quality of sleep is poor (ie we don't spend enough time in deep and REM sleep), then we will not feel rested. If this trend continues over time, both our health and performance will suffer.

Find your rhythm

We discussed our natural or evolutionary sleep/wake cycle (the circadian rhythm) in Chapter Six. That cycle or rhythm remains unchanged. The sun still rises and sets and our hormones that govern sleep still work in the same way. The problem is that modern life has intervened and disrupted our ability to follow that natural rhythm.

So, how can we reset it? The best way of resetting our circadian rhythm is to get exposure to morning sunlight and natural light throughout the day, as much as possible.[86] Getting a good night's sleep depends on sending the right signals to our brain so that our body produces the right hormones, at the right times. The other factor is to avoid sending mixed signals to our brain. We discussed in Chapter Six that white or blue light (those prevalent in modern lighting and our device screens) mimic the light of the rising sun and, therefore, confuse our brains when we are exposed to them late in the evening.

Get some exposure to sunlight in the morning, and as much as possible throughout the day. Our circadian rhythm is highly reliant on natural light to keep it calibrated. The problem is that we are generally stuck indoors most of the day and have little exposure to natural light. Spend at least 5 minutes getting the morning light into your eyes. It doesn't need to be direct sunlight, so don't stare directly into the sun, but just being outside in the ambient light means that you're getting exposure to the right wavelength of light. To make it even more time-efficient, do some walking, stretching or yoga outside to kick off your daily movement as well. The same applies throughout the day. Studies have shown that getting enough natural sunlight during the day helps to optimise melatonin production.[87]

Create a routine

Once you've dialled in your circadian rhythm, there are a number of sleep hygiene tips and tricks that will help you to further improve the quality of your sleep. Try them to see which ones work for you by noticing the impact they have on your sleep.

Consistent sleep/wake pattern

Our bodies crave consistency when it comes to sleep. If we surrender ourselves to the natural sleep rhythm (ie based on the signals to our brain from natural sunlight), we would go to bed at the same time at night and wake up at the same time in the morning without the need for an alarm clock. Not many people achieve this natural consistency these days, primarily due to light pollution and other factors such as stress and poor eating and movement habits. But we can re-train ourselves to have a regular, consistent sleep pattern. Finding or resetting our circadian rhythm through exposure to natural light is the first step. The next step is to stick to a regular sleep and waking time.

Based on our sleep cycles discussed in Chapter Six, our bedtime should be before 11 o'clock to ensure that we hit the more prolonged, deep sleep cycles that occur before midnight, and then add seven-and-a-half to 8 hours to that bedtime. If you have to get up for work before seven in the morning, then you will need to push your bedtime back accordingly. Ideally, this sleep routine should be consistent throughout the week. Inevitably, many people short-sleep during the week (ie get less than the required 7.5–8 hours) and then try to make it up on the weekend. This phenomenon is known as 'social jetlag' and it has been shown to have negative health consequences.[88] Studies have also shown that the problem is more closely related to reducing the amount of sleep during the week, rather than trying to catch up on the weekend.

So, pick a sleep/wake time and try to stick with it. As tempting as it is to sleep in on the weekends, try to avoid it. You will benefit from better overall sleep once you get into the routine and will also have much higher energy and concentration levels during the day.

Move during the day

This is another good example of the interaction between different health drivers. Doing moderate to vigorous movement for at least 20 to 30 minutes per day has been shown to promote deeper sleep at night.[89] As discussed, exercise can also help to manage stress, and lowering stress is a major factor in getting a good night's sleep. Avoid strenuous exercise too close to bedtime – within 1-2 hours – as this can have the effect of waking you up (cortisol and endorphins produced during exercise promote wakefulness). Exercise can also raise your core body temperature, whereas sleep requires your temperature to drop (see more below). Going for a walk after dinner is an excellent moderate movement activity that won't spike endorphins but will put you in a good position for sleep.

Avoid large meals before sleeping

There's an old proverb when it comes to the amount of food we should eat during the day: 'Eat breakfast like a king, lunch like a prince and dinner like a pauper.' There is evidence that this strategy is good for maintaining your ideal body composition,[90] but it's also sound advice to follow for ensuring a good night's sleep. Eating too much too close to bedtime can disturb our sleep in several ways. Firstly, digestion requires a lot of energy and so it puts our sleeping body under stress. Secondly, if we eat stimulating foods like chocolate, or even refined carbs, it can keep us up or make it difficult to reach the deeper stages of sleep. Finally, eating refined carbs (sugars) can make you wake up in the middle of the night craving more carbs (aka 'having the munchies').

Eat your last meal 2-3 hours before going to sleep. This way, your stomach will be pretty empty, so you won't feel bloated, but you also won't feel hungry. Try to eat a balanced meal with protein, some fat and complex carbs. This will leave you feeling satiated throughout the night and help you avoid the munchies.

Avoid drinking alcohol or caffeine close to bedtime

We all enjoy a nice glass of wine in the evening from time to time, and some of us even associate it with winding down before going to bed. You may even feel that it helps you to sleep – that it 'knocks you out'. The problem is just that. Alcohol is a sedative. It makes us feel sleepy and even puts us to 'sleep' faster, but we're actually not sleeping – we're sedated – which is a different state entirely. In the earlier phases of sleep, it inhibits us from getting into deep sleep, and in the later phases, as the alcohol starts to wear off, it interferes with our REM sleep.[91] This is why we often wake up feeling unrested after drinking alcohol late in the evening.

Caffeine, on the other hand, blocks the process for feeling sleepy, which is why it's such a popular substance! The problem is that caffeine has a half-life of around 4-6 hours and, therefore, if you consume caffeine at six in the evening, you still have around half of the volume in your system at midnight. Having any significant amount of caffeine in your system when you're trying to sleep is counterproductive, and the effect is to prevent you from reaching the deeper stages of sleep until all of the caffeine is out of your system, which might be well into the morning, depending on how late you had your last cup.[92]

Drinking alcohol and caffeine in moderation is ok for our health, and several studies have demonstrated some health benefits of drinking small amounts of red wine and caffeine. However, both have a significant impact on sleep and therefore the timing and amount consumed should be closely monitored. Notice how it makes you feel the next morning. If you wake up not feeling rested, chances are you need to moderate your consumption of one or both.

Set the right environment for sleep

As with any habit, setting the right environment to build healthy sleeping habits is crucial. Your bedroom should be a place for sleeping (and having sexy time!), not working or entertainment (having a TV in your bedroom is a really bad idea – see above discussion on the disruptiveness of blue-wave light). Limit the clutter or anything that will distract you from the business of sleeping. Try to eliminate *all* sources of light from the room. Our eyes are particularly sensitive to light (even when they're closed, including any red or green ones from chargers, etc.). Blackout curtains work well, but you can also wear eye shades if they don't annoy you. These are also good when travelling, or on a flight. Temperature is also a critical factor for ensuring deep sleep. Like bears and other hibernating animals, we need a cooler environment for good quality sleep. Our core temperature actually has to drop by 1.5 to 2 degrees Celsius to ensure good sleep. The recommended temperature in your bedroom for sleep is therefore between 15 to 19 degrees Celsius (or 60 to 67 degrees Fahrenheit). Any hotter than that makes it difficult for your body to get to the necessary temperature for sound sleep.

Have a regular wind-down routine

We do it for our kids but, somehow, we forget the importance of a bedtime routine for ourselves. It's a mindset issue. We benefit from getting our brain and body ready for sleep. A bedtime routine can include a warm bath with Epsom salts and maybe a few drops of lavender oil. This is an excellent way of relaxing the body and mind to get ready for sleep. Reading a good book (not a scary one!) usually helps people to relax. A powerful exercise is to keep a journal by your bed. Make a note of anything that has happened during the day that you are grateful for. You can also use it to note what your priorities are for the next day, so that you can draw a line under them and get them off your mind while you sleep. In the event that you have something that still wakes you up at night, you can write down ideas that pop into your head so that your mind can relax again and let you go back to sleep!

Breathe!

We've talked a lot about breathing already, but the simple power of breathing can't be overstated, and is particularly relevant for a good night's sleep. As discussed in Chapter Eight, calm, deep breathing signals to our bodies that we are safe and puts us into a parasympathetic mode. In the case of sleep, this is obviously important. We've all been there when we're trying to fall asleep, but we're still stressed out about what happened at work or worrying about the workload of tomorrow (see the note on journaling above). We know that stress produces cortisol, which, in turn, disrupts our sleep. Using our breath to get us into the 'rest and digest' state will help to lower cortisol levels.

Sleep for performance

We've talked a lot about the important role that sleep plays for our health, including regulating blood pressure, controlling appetite, regulating hormones, etc, but what is less well appreciated is the impact of sleep on our performance. The negative effects of lack of sleep on performance are pretty obvious. Try staying awake in a boring meeting or focusing on the task at hand if you've gotten too little sleep the night before. But, the list of performance enhancements from getting a good quantity and quality of sleep are pretty impressive. Let's take the most impactful of them in turn.

Memory processing

Sleep affects our ability to learn new information and to remember it. Without adequate sleep, we struggle to focus on the new information, making it difficult to take in and, ultimately, remember it. Poor sleep also affects our judgement and tends to colour the way we interpret new information. Having good sleep, on the other hand, enables us to take in new information more quickly and to retain it better. While awake, new information is stored in our short-term memory and it's only while we sleep that it gets transferred to, and processed in, the areas of our brain that deal with long-term memory. Studies have shown that people who have slept well have much better memory retention and faster retrieval times following new learning than those that lacked adequate sleep when learning new information.[93]

Problem-solving and creativity

We've all heard the phrase, 'Let's sleep on it,' when we encounter a particularly difficult problem where the solution is not obvious. There is now a body of scientific evidence to support this. Studies have found that after working on a difficult problem, like navigating a maze, those that got a good night's sleep significantly improved their ability to solve the problem compared to the control group who were sleep deprived. The participants in these studies had their sleep monitored, and it turns out that when we dream (ie enter REM sleep), our brains continue to work on the problem and combine new information and previous experiences in novel ways to solve the problem.[94]

Emotional healing

We all encounter stressful, sometimes even embarrassing, events during the day. You may have noticed that these events usually seem a little less stressful or embarrassing after a good night's sleep, and even seem to wane further as time passes. This is due to a process that occurs while we sleep, or more precisely, while we dream. It is thought to involve a decrease in activity in the region of the brain associated with fear (the amygdala) and an increase in the prefrontal cortex (the rational part of the brain).[95] It's a bit like having your own, personal psychologist while you sleep, whispering, 'It's OK. Everything's gonna be alright!'

Take action

- Get natural light into your eyes within an hour of waking up, ideally combining it with some outdoor activity, like walking.

- Move during the day but avoid vigorous movement right before bed.

- Eat a small balanced meal 2–3 hours before bed and avoid alcohol and caffeine in the evening.

- Find your own ideal bedtime/wake-up time and stick to it. Make sure you sleep a few hours *before* midnight too.

- Create a relaxing wind-down routine before bed: bath, book, camomile tea, meditation, breathing exercise, stretching and switch off your devices.

- Keep a bedside journal. Writing down your thoughts can help you clear your mind and limit your stress, which will improve the quality of your sleep.

13
F – Fasten Your Seatbelt

You are almost ready for takeoff. We promise that the journey will be fun and full of new discoveries about yourself, your body and your mind. It will be exciting to see the changes and experience feeling better and more productive every week. We do have to warn you that there will almost certainly be unexpected turbulence along the way. You can also expect delays, and you will probably need to do some in-flight course corrections as you find yourself on an occasional detour. So, fasten your seatbelt and enjoy the ride!

Commit for life

Health should be non-negotiable. It is our most precious asset and is the key driver of our performance, success and, ultimately, wellbeing. This is the mindset we need to foster to make health an integral part of our daily lives. Without it, what do we have? There's an old saying: 'A person with their health has a thousand dreams. A person without it has only one.' We tend to take our health for granted, until we suffer a significant illness. We think we're indestructible, until it's clear that we're not. We get caught up in the daily grind and lose sight of our real priorities. By taking care of our health, the rest takes care of itself. When we're truly healthy, we can weather the temporary storms of life without letting them blow us completely off course. We begin to truly appreciate the marvel that our bodies are and the blessings we receive each day. We're better able to prioritise and take care of the things that really matter.

Health is not a single destination. It's a lifelong journey. Now that you're buckled up, you're ready to start your wellbeing adventure.

Enjoy the ride

Perhaps the most important criterion in building a healthy lifestyle is this: have fun! Life is far too short, so we may as well try to find things that make us happy *and* healthy. There's a joke where a doctor says to his patient, 'Look, Paddy, the smokin' and the drinkin' are killing you. If you give them up, chances are you'll live a couple of years longer.' And Paddy replies, 'That may be so, Doctor, but I'll be pretty feckin' miserable in the meantime!' OK, it's a terrible joke, but the point is, unless we enjoy what we're doing to build healthy habits, we're not going to stick with them. As we discussed with the habit loop, if the reward is not there, the loop does not close and no habit is formed. We end up relying on willpower to stay on track and, ultimately, our willpower is limited and will not sustain ongoing changes.

Being healthy is not about hardship. It's about a higher quality of life. If we think of it as giving our bodies a gift when we adopt healthy habits under the four drivers of health, then it shifts our mindset. For example, instead of seeing walking as 'inconvenient and not time-efficient', or as something we 'have to do' to be healthy, look at it as providing our bodies with the movement they need to sustain our circulatory systems. We're assisting our lymphatic systems to clear unhealthy toxins from our bodies that would otherwise be stored in our fat cells and cause all sorts of problems down the road. We're taking in more oxygen, which powers every cell in our bodies, increasing our energy and focus. We're reducing our stress hormones and balancing our blood sugar by controlling insulin levels, while at the same time triggering the release of happy hormones such as dopamine and endorphins. How inspiring and motivating is that?

On movement, do what you love and what challenges you. Don't go to the gym if you hate it. Swim in the sea if that's what floats your boat. If yoga is your thing, be passionate about it. If you like running, make it yours. At the same time, look for fun ways to incorporate the other movement types into your daily routine. Be creative and find things that bring you joy and that you can do anywhere. Try skipping rope. Yes, that old childhood favourite. It's an excellent way to get your heart rate up and you can throw the skipping rope into your bag when you're travelling or going on holiday. An exercise band (essentially a big rubber band) amps up your callisthenics (bodyweight movements); it's a great way to build strength and is also portable.

When it comes to food, eating healthy does not mean sacrificing taste. Quite the opposite. We have a good friend who once said to us, 'Healthy food doesn't taste good.' This is a common misconception, which relates more to the fact that many people associate eating 'healthy' with having to make sacrifices and 'give stuff up'. If you follow the principles from Chapter Ten, not only do you *not* have to sacrifice taste, in fact, the flavours will far exceed anything the food industry can manufacture (although they do their best to trick our tastebuds so that we eat more of their so-called 'food').

Although we have come to rely on 'convenience' foods due to our fast-paced lives, we can rediscover the joy of preparing our own food – and have fun in the process. Preparing your own food can be deeply satisfying and healing. It will take time to get the hang of it if you are just starting out, but cooking doesn't need to be time- or labour-intensive. As a bonus, invite friends and colleagues over from time to time to show off your culinary skills. You will also get a hit of oxytocin, the 'love' or 'social' hormone. This acts as a further reward, which embeds the habits of cooking and eating healthy even more deeply.

Finally, sleep. There are still some of us who genuinely enjoy sleep and don't see it as something to be sacrificed at the altar of success. Let's all get there! Have fun with your sleep routine. Look forward to that bubble bath, or the cup of camomile tea, or curling up with your favourite book before you drift off into a deep, restorative sleep. It's difficult to stress out about something you enjoy. Practise your breathing and other relaxation techniques to send a signal to your brain that you're safe and all is well in the world. Leave any stressful thoughts in your bedside journal, to be tackled the next day when you're fully rested.

Course correct

Life happens. Even with the best of intentions, we all face headwinds that can knock us off course. We then tend to resort to old habits and patterns that seem appropriate at the time, but are, ultimately, damaging to our health and performance. When we notice that we're slipping into autopilot, it's important to go back to our core principles. Bringing awareness to the situation enables us to short circuit the bad behaviour, turn off autopilot and take back control. When the 'flight' doesn't go to plan, it's OK, because we have the tools and procedures to course correct. No point beating ourselves up. Take control over what we can control, and the rest will take care of itself. Remember, it's not about getting it right 100% of the time. It's good to strive for perfection, but better to be consistent and directionally correct.

Here are some examples of times when it can be difficult to stay on track, and what we can do to manage the challenges and quickly get back on course.

Travelling for work

People working in the airline industry tend to travel *a lot*, and travelling is one of the most common ways of falling off the wagon. We get up early for flights and then fight traffic and crowds at the airport. We sit around when the flight is delayed and eat crap 'food' (let's be honest, airport food is not exactly healthy). When we get on the flight, space is limited (unless you're in business- or first-class) and it's difficult to manage any kind of movement. Being at altitude exacerbates circulatory issues, which is why deep vein thrombosis is a serious issue, so it really is important to find ways to move regularly.[96] Then there's jet lag, sleeping in strange beds and the stress of doing business after being subjected to all of the above! Often, being away for a significant period of time or having a lot of such travel can totally knock us off track. Before we know it, it feels like we're back at square one in relation to our health.

What can we do about it? First, having the right mindset is critical. It starts with recognising that travel is a part of our lives, so we need to plan around it or we can't perform at our best in these circumstances. For example, when it comes to nutrition, if you plan ahead, you can prepare healthy snacks to have on hand in case it's not possible to find real food at the airport or on the flight. When you become comfortable with the concept of fasting, you can also prepare yourself in advance and simply fast until you reach your destination and a source of real food. Always remember to hydrate, especially at altitude, where we tend to dehydrate more quickly (drinking alcohol at altitude exacerbates this). On movement, do what you can. Maximise the intensity of your movement while in transit. For example, walk briskly and don't be afraid to carry your bags to add a strength component – remember the earlier example of the New York hotel room attendants!

And, finally, sleep. Our sleep can be seriously disrupted while travelling. Jet lag is a constant companion of the busy traveller. The problem with jet lag is that we leave our circadian rhythm at the departure gate, and it takes our bodies time to adjust to our new time zone. Flight crew tend to have the best strategies for dealing with jet lag. Whether it's starting to adjust their bodies to the new time zone before they travel, or using the 10.30 rule (ie if you arrive at your hotel before 10.30am, go to sleep for a couple of hours; if it's after 10.30, then try to stay up until it's bedtime in the new time zone). Sleeping in a strange bed can also disrupt our sleep. It triggers an evolutionary defence mechanism whereby we don't sleep too deeply in case we need to respond to some threat. There's actually a term for it – 'first-night effect' (FNE) – and it involves one hemisphere of our brain remaining more alert while we sleep.[97]

JIM'S STORY

I had a long-haul flight from Amsterdam to Chicago recently that involved a time difference of 7 hours. I was also transiting through Iceland, which further complicated things. In preparation for the trip, I started to adjust my sleep time the week before so that it reduced the impact at the other end. When I got on the flight, I set my watch to the new time zone and made a plan around what to eat and when to try to sleep, again, to start adjusting to the destination. While on board, I got up every hour or so to walk down the aisle and also found a spot to do some micro-movements and stretching. I felt a bit self-conscious at first, but I could swear that some of the passengers started doing the same after the first few times! At the other end, I used the 10.30 rule. I arrived at my hotel in the afternoon, so I stayed up until it was bed time in Chicago. I also went outside for a walk to get some natural light. Finally, I tried to stick closely to my normal bedtime routine, including some light stretching just before bed and reading my book. The combination of all these efforts significantly reduced the impact of jet lag.

Holidays

Holidays are always a difficult time for sticking to healthy habits. Whether it's spending time with family or staying at a nice hotel or resort, temptations are everywhere. Breakfasts are lavish, the poolside menu is mouth-watering, and the BBQ dinners are irresistible. The little food devil in your head is constantly reminding you that, 'You've paid for it; it's the *only* time you can finally unwind and enjoy life; you'll go on a strict diet and run every morning *immediately* after you return home...' Sound familiar? Here's the reality. These are common excuses we make to justify unhealthy habits. 'Oh, but what is life if I can't enjoy a glass of wine and a big steak occasionally?' Right? You absolutely can, and here's how. Don't feel obliged to eat everything on the buffet table just because you have FOMO.[98] You will be back next year, or you'll go to an even better resort. Mind your portions. Since when do you have an omelette with sausages, pancakes with maple syrup, a croissant, yoghurt with granola *and* a bowl of fruit for breakfast? Eat mindfully and pay attention to your body's signals. Drink responsibly. If you are going to have a glass of wine, drink it at lunchtime, instead of in the evening. This will ensure that your sleep is not disrupted (see discussion from Chapter Twelve).

Keeping up with a good movement routine while on holiday will also help mitigate any overeating. Go for a brisk walk after meals and try to plan some activities. Swimming, hiking and playing sports are all good options. Don't forget to take your skipping rope and exercise band with you. Pro tip: always try to stay at a hotel that has a decent gym so you can get some strength training in!

NATASA'S STORY

Having lived in Abu Dhabi for years, we became used to the amazing buffets in the hotels and regularly went for brunch in some of them. The quality of the food was excellent, but there was so much of it! We are big fans of Middle Eastern cuisine, so we would indulge in all the mezze, such as the various types of hummus, moutabal, muhammara, pickled vegetables and salads of all sorts. Then came the main course of freshly caught fish and amazing grilled meats. And, finally, the dessert... Gorgeous, healthy fruit and those irresistible tiny cakes and pastries – bite-sized, really. By the time we'd finished, we needed someone to roll us out of the place!

Sound familiar? It's taken us years to reach the point of managing these situations (and even now we don't get it right all of the time). Ask yourself why you're eating this food. The first point should always be 'to promote my health' and, as a secondary consideration, 'to enjoy this good quality food'. If the priority is health, you will be mindful of things like what to eat, and in what proportion (remember the principles from Chapter Ten). Eating sweet desserts (which should always be limited, in any event) before going to bed means that they will spike your insulin and the calories will go straight to your fat cells. If all else fails, go for a brisk walk afterwards to stabilise your blood sugar levels!

Change in life circumstances

Major changes in our lives can seriously throw us off track from a health perspective. Changing jobs, getting married, getting divorced, loss of a loved one: all of these can throw a wrench in our daily routine and, if we're not careful, before we know it, we have lost momentum and slipped back into unhealthy habits. Stress often plays a major role in these cases, so it's important to go back to our strategies for managing stress and maintaining a healthy mindset, which will stop us from slipping too far. Always remember that health is the priority. Being healthy will help us to adjust to our new reality and to thrive in our new circumstances.

Some practical strategies for managing these types of situations is to start to re-establish your daily routines around the four drivers as soon as possible. It will also be particularly important to practise your formal and informal mindfulness to help keep things in perspective during these times. On the nutrition front, figure out where the best sources of wholesome foods are – these may be the farmers' markets or good bio-supermarkets (and some great restaurants for special occasions). On movement, if you've had to leave your old gym or sports club, quickly do your research to find a replacement. Find your new tribe if it's no longer feasible to share your experiences with your old one.

Change in life stages (aka ageing)

Getting older is inevitable, but maintaining a healthy lifestyle based on all four drivers of health can slow down the process and allow us to live our best life at any stage. We discussed the ageing curve earlier and saw that we can push it out (ie avoid the zone of dysfunctionality) when we start to adopt a healthy lifestyle. Remaining active and following our health strategy is crucial, no matter our age. We will, of course, need to adjust our routine to reflect our capabilities, but the core principles and habits that we've developed remain the same. For example, we may not be able to lift as heavy a load as we get older, but we certainly don't stop lifting altogether. In fact, strength training becomes even more important as we age, because it slows the rate of muscle mass and bone density loss.

One of the top causes of death when we reach our seventies and eighties is complications due to falls.[99] Loss of balance, weaker muscles and brittle bones due to inadequate exercise and poor diet are a recipe for serious injury from a fall, which in itself can be fatal or can lead to a long, slow decline in our health. It doesn't need to be so. Adjusting our exercise and nutrition programmes to match our changing needs will help us to stay in peak health and enjoy our best years.

Take action

- Get hooked on health. It is truly your greatest treasure.

- Focus on the long game. Make consistent, micro-changes that lead to macro-transformations.

- Have fun, be grateful and do more of what you love.

- Prepare for the inevitable challenges and changes. Use the tools and framework to adjust and get back on track.

- Never stop growing, learning and loving.

Conclusion

We hope you now feel ready to embark on the journey to a happier, healthier and more productive self. In *Ready for TAKEOFF!* we have shared our own experiences and provided you with tools and techniques to not only start writing your own wellness story, but also to set you on an upward spiral that will carry you to new heights of health and performance.

Our own journeys started with a change of mindset, borne from painful experiences dealing with stressful careers and the resulting unhealthy habits we unconsciously developed over the years. It was when we finally uncovered our individual Whys, our deep emotional reasons for wanting to change, that we finally started to crack the code. With the buy-in from our heads and our hearts, the journey became one of discovering the components for achieving true health and its impact on performance. We might have similar family and career goals as a couple, but as a male and a female we have different body needs, fitness levels and, consequently, health goals. The TAKE-OFF model makes it easy for us to stay on course and achieve our goals both as individuals and as a couple.

We are continuously rewriting our wellness stories as we learn more about our bodies and minds along the way. The limits are almost non-existent – at least, not in the sense we used to perceive them. Becoming older doesn't mean you have to give up on yourself and accept declining cognitive and physical performance. We know this for a fact.[100] By making conscious choices and taking small, consistent steps each and every day with a strong Why in our hearts and science-based information in our heads, we can not only stave off deterioration, but take our wellbeing and performance to whole new levels.

What will your wellness story look like? What will you start doing *today* to have a better tomorrow? Where will your journey lead you? Don't aim for perfection; aim for consistency. Show up every day and take one small action. That's what matters. With time, you will build those small actions into powerful new habits.

It takes all of the decision-making out of the process and, together with the contents of this book, will give you enough information to get buy-in from your logical brain. The individual steps will challenge you enough to keep you motivated, without being so onerous that you're tempted to give up. Each change in one driver will have positive effects in the others and slowly, over time, you will start to feel that upwards spiral. You will also begin to notice the positive changes in your life: increased energy levels, improved focus, a better mood and positive outlook, lower stress levels, absence of pain and anxiety, etc. These are your rewards from a habit-building perspective. Be conscious of them. Write them down. Associate them with the new habits you're introducing.

As a bonus, we have provided a QR code in the Resources section, which includes the Reset part of our signature Ready for TAKEOFF Programme, together with some other helpful materials. This first six-week cycle is just to get you started. Once you reset your mind and body and the healthy habits start to show results, you can then increase the intensity of activities in each of the four drivers. This will challenge you further and result in even higher levels of health and performance.

Let's do a quick pre-flight check to make sure we are ready for the journey:

- ☑ Turn off autopilot
- ☑ Address your stress
- ☑ Know your 'Why'

- ☑ Eat yourself healthy
- ☑ Optimise your movement
- ☑ Fix your sleep
- ☑ Fasten your seatbelt!

Now you're ready for takeoff. Enjoy the ride!

Resources

Please scan this QR code or click the link below for more resources and practical applications of the TAKEOFF model, including the first six weeks of The TAKEOFF Programme to help you reset.

https://wellnesstory.world/book-resources

Notes

1 AJ Mrazek, MD Mrazek et al, Measuring High Performance: The High Performance Indicator Development and Validation (High Performance Institute, 2019), www.highperformanceinstitute.com/blog/measurement, accessed 21 March 2023

2 TEDx Talks, 'The stories we choose to live: Michael Margolis at TEDxFurmanU', www.youtube.com/watch?v=fwlT6eUpTNM&ab_channel=TEDxTalks, accessed 4 April 2023

3 S Sinek, *Start With Why: How great leaders inspire everyone to take action* (Penguin, 2011)

4 Appreciative Inquiry is a philosophy and a positive psychology framework. It is essentially a strength-based change management and leadership development tool that helps individuals, teams and organisations to become the best versions of themselves. See https://appreciativeinquiry.champlain.edu/learn/appreciative-inquiry-introduction for further information

5 J Watzek, SM Pope and SF Brosnan, 'Capuchin and rhesus monkeys but not humans show cognitive flexibility in an optional-switch task', *Scientific Reports* (2019), https://doi.org/10.1038/s41598-019-49658-0

6 M Zhu, T Wang et al, 'Genetic risk for overall cancer and the benefit of adherence to a healthy lifestyle', *Cancer Research*, 81:17 (2021), https://doi.org/10.1158/0008-5472. CAN-21-0836

7 PA O'Keefe, CS Dweck and GM Walton, 'Implicit theories of interest: Finding your passion or developing it?', *Psychological Science* (6 September 2018), https://doi. org/10.1177/0956797618780643

8 At the time of writing (2023), France, Italy, Ireland, Portugal, Slovakia, Canada and Belgium have implemented such laws.

9 DL Schacter and DT Gilbert, DM Wegner, *Psychology* (2nd Edition) (Worth, 2011)

10 D Burnett, *The Idiot Brain: A neuroscientist explains what your head is really up to* (Guardian Faber, 2016)

11 Mayo Clinic Staff, 'Chronic stress puts your health at risk', Mayo Clinic (8 July 2021), www.mayoclinic.org/healthy-lifestyle/stress-management/in-depth/stress/art-20046037, accessed 10 March 2023

12 Ibid

13 C Duhigg, *The Power of Habit: Why we do what we do in life and business* (Random House, 2012)

14 KP Madore and AD Wagner, 'Multicosts of multitasking', Cerebrum Dana Foundation (5 April 2019), www.dana.org/article/multicosts-of-multitasking, accessed 13 February 2023

15 C Duhigg, *The Power of Habit: Why we do what we do in life and business* (Random House, 2012)

16 M Ben-Dor, R Sirtoli and R Barkai, 'The evolution of the human trophic level during the Pleistocene', *Yearbook of Physical Anthropology* (2021), https://doi.org/10.1002/ajpa.24247

17 With the exception of honey, which had its own challenges in terms of finding and getting it.

18 D Swain-Lenz et al, 'Comparative analyses of chromatin landscape in white adipose tissue suggest humans may have less beigeing potential than other primates', *Genome Biology and Evolution*, 11:7 (2019), https://doi.org/10.1093/gbe/evz134

19 Rungeni editors, 'Running calories calculator – the calories you burn running', Rungeni (4 February 2020), www.rungeni.com/calories-burned-running-calc, accessed 13 February 2023

20 Autophagy is the body's natural process of self-cleaning, when it gets rid of damaged proteins and other dysfunctional cells to regenerate. Yoshinori Ohsumi won a Nobel prize in 2016 for discovering autophagy.

21 'Obesity and overweight', WHO (9 June 2021), www.who.int/news-room/fact-sheets/detail/obesity-and-overweight, accessed 13 February 2023

22 Note that saturated fats themselves are not bad; it's the amount and way they're combined in processed foods that make them a problem.

23 'Guidance: Health matters: Obesity and the food environment', Gov.UK (31 March 2017), www.gov.uk/government/publications/health-matters-obesity-and-the-food-environment/health-matters-obesity-and-the-food-environment, accessed 13 February 2023

24 J Sonnenburg and S Sonnenburg, *The Good Gut: Taking control of your weight, your mood and your long-term health* (Penguin, 2016). Interesting fact: before a baby is born, its intestinal tract is completely sterile and is only colonised by bacteria during and after birth. The way we are born (vaginally or C-section) and whether we are breastfed has a significant impact on our gut flora and our resistance to illnesses at later stages of life.

25 C Zimmer, 'How many cells are in your body?', *National Geographic* (23 October 2013), www.nationalgeographic.com/science/article/how-many-cells-are-in-your-body, accessed 13 February 2023

26 SP Wiertsema et al, 'The Interplay between the gut microbiome and the immune system in the context of infectious diseases throughout life and the role of nutrition in optimizing treatment strategies', *Nutrients* (March 2021), https://doi.org/10.3390/nu13030886

27 M Carabotti et al, 'The gut-brain axis: Interactions between enteric microbiota, central and enteric nervous systems', *Annals of Gastroenterology*, 28:2 (2015), pp20–209, www.ncbi.nlm.nih.gov/pmc/articles/PMC4367209, accessed 13 February 2023

28 J Sonnenburg and S Sonnenburg, *The Good Gut: Taking control of your weight, your mood and your long-term health* (Penguin, 2016)

29 For the purposes of this discussion, we use the terms carbohydrates and sugars interchangeably, because carbohydrates break down into sugars, and the sugars convert into glucose in the bloodstream.

30 The process is called glycation and it occurs when the excess glucose interacts with protein molecules in our blood causing loss of elasticity of our skin, joint tissue and even blood vessels. The process of inflammation leads our immune systems to overreact to a perceived threat.

31 S Rahman, 'Role of insulin in health and disease: An update', *International Journal of Molecular Science* (15 June 2021), https://doi.org/10.3390/ijms22126403

32 'Insulin resistance', Cleveland Clinic (no date), https://my.clevelandclinic.org/health/diseases/22206-insulin-resistance, accessed 13 February 2023

33 DM Bramble and DE Lieberman, 'Endurance running and the evolution of homo', *Nature, 432* (2004) pp345–352, www.nature.com/articles/nature03052, accessed 13 February 2023

34 H Pontzner, 'Humans evolved to exercise', *Scientific American* (1 January 2019), www.scientificamerican.com/article/humans-evolved-to-exercise, accessed 13 February 2023

35 Ibid.

36 Interesting fact: Natasa has at times recorded in the range of 5,000 steps during the process of cooking big meals. Depending on the meal, there may also be some lifting (turkey, anyone?) or climbing – some of the shelves in the pantry require a small stepladder. It all adds up!

37 'Physical activity', WHO (5 October 2022), www.who.int/news-room/fact-sheets/detail/physical-activity, accessed 13 February 2023

38 'Guidelines on physical activity and sedentary behaviour', WHO (25 November 2020), www.who.int/publications/i/item/9789240015128, accessed 13 February 2023

39 The National Human Genome Research Institute defines mitochondria as 'membrane-bound cell organelles (mitochondrion, singular) that generate most of the chemical energy needed to power the cell's biochemical reactions. Chemical energy produced by the mitochondria is stored in a small molecule called adenosine triphosphate (ATP).' Source: 'Mitochondria', NIH (updated 9 February 2023), www.genome.gov/genetics-glossary/Mitochondria, accessed 13 February 2023

40 R Mualem et al, 'The effect of movement on cognitive performance', *Frontiers in Public Health, 6* (2018), https://doi.org/10.3389/fpubh.2018.00100

41 MA Tosches et al, 'Melatonin signalling controls circadian swimming behavior in marine zooplankton', *Cell Press*, 159:1 (2014), pp46–57, https://doi.org/10.1016/j. cell.2014.07.042

42 The record for going without sleep is 11 days and 25 minutes, which was set by seventeen-year-old Randy Gardner in 1963. Interestingly, the *Guinness Book of World Records* subsequently removed sleep deprivation from permitted record attempts, given its negative health effects.

43 Institute of Medicine (US) Committee on Sleep Medicine and Research, HR Colten and BM Altevogt (eds), *Sleep Disorders and Sleep Deprivation: An unmet public health problem* (National Academies Press (US), 2006), www.ncbi. nlm.nih.gov/books/NBK19958/#

44 This is the reason for strict, worldwide regulations on minimum rest requirements for pilots and cabin crew.

45 'Seeking solutions: How COVID-19 changed sleep around the world', Philips (2021), www.usa.philips.com/c-dam/ b2c/master/experience/smartsleep/world-sleep-day/2021/philips-world-sleep-day-2021-report.pdf, accessed 13 February 2023

46 A chemical called adenosine, which is a by-product of energy production in our brain, actually causes that sleepy feeling, or 'sleep pressure', as it builds up in the late evening. We can therefore feel desperately tired and want to sleep, but other mechanisms (like the presence of cortisol or caffeine) are working against us.

47 'Sleep and chronic disease', CDC (reviewed 13 September 2022), www.cdc.gov/sleep/about_sleep/chronic_disease. html, accessed 13 February 2023

48 M Walker, *Why We Sleep: The new science of sleep and dreams* (Penguin, 2018)

49 K Nunez and K Lamoreux, 'What is the purpose of sleep?' *Healthline* (20 July 2020), www.healthline.com/health/why-do-we-sleep, accessed 13 February 2023

50 Lack of adequate sleep has been linked to a buildup of these substances in the brain, which is thought to be a major contributor to certain types of dementia, including Alzheimer's.

51 Precise measurements have shown that the human circadian rhythm averages 24.18 hours. CA Czeisler et al, 'Stability, precision and near-24-hour period of the human

circadian pacemaker', *Science*, 284 (1999), https://doi.
org/10.1126/science.284.5423.2177

52   'How sleep works: Your sleep/wake cycle', NIH (24 March
2022), www.nhlbi.nih.gov/health/sleep/sleep-wake-cycle,
accessed 13 February 2023

53   If you've ever been woken up in the middle of a deep sleep
phase, you'll understand the point.

54   MA Killingsworth and DT Gilbert, 'A wandering mind is
an unhappy mind', *Science*, 330 (2010), www.science.org/
doi/10.1126/science.1192439

55   A definition and expanded explanation of VUCA can be
found at www.techtarget.com/whatis/definition/VUCA-
volatility-uncertainty-complexity-and-ambiguity, accessed
13 February 2023

56   E Seppälä, 'How meditation benefits CEOs', HBR
(14 December 2015), https://hbr.org/2015/12/how-
meditation-benefits-ceos, accessed 13 February 2023

57   AA Taren et al, 'Dispositional mindfulness co-varies with
smaller amygdala and caudate volumes in community
adults', *PLoS One* (22 May 2013), https://doi.org/10.1371/
journal.pone.0064574

58   S Mittleman, *Slow Burn: Burn fat faster by exercising slower*
(William Morrow Paperbacks, 2001)

59   CE Ackerman, 'Mindfulness-based stress reduction: The
ultimate MBSR guide', PositivePsychology.com (12 January
2023), https://positivepsychology.com/mindfulness-
based-stress-reduction-mbsr, accessed 13 February 2023

60   W Shakespeare, *Hamlet*, Act II, Scene 2

61   AF Arnsten, 'Catecholamine and second messenger
influences on prefrontal cortical networks of
"representational knowledge": A rational bridge between
genetics and the symptoms of mental illness', *Cerebral
Cortex*, 17 (suppl_1) (2007), ppi6–i15, https://doi.
org/10.1093/cercor/bhm033

62   J Loehr and T Schwartz, *The Power of Full Engagement:
Managing energy, not time, is the key to high performance and
personal renewal* (Free Press Paperbacks, 2003)

63   'Stress and health', *The Nutrition Source* (no date), www.
hsph.harvard.edu/nutritionsource/stress-and-health,
accessed 13 February 2023

64   S Sinek, *Start with Why: How great leaders inspire everyone to
take action* (Penguin, 2011)

65   *The Croods* (DreamWorks, 2013)

66 D Cooperrider and D Whitney, *A Positive Revolution in Change: Appreciative inquiry* (Berrett-Koehler Publishers, 2005)

67 C Sissons, 'What is the average percentage of water in the human body?' *Medical News Today* (27 May 2020), www.medicalnewstoday.com/articles/what-percentage-of-the-human-body-is-water, accessed 13 February 2023

68 CE Cherpak, 'Mindful eating: A review of how the stress-digestion-mindfulness triad may modulate and improve gastrointestinal and digestive function, integrative medicine', *A Clinician's Journal*, 18:4 (2019), www.ncbi.nlm.nih.gov/pmc/articles/PMC7219460, accessed 13 February 2023

69 Actual words of one of our dear friends and ex-colleague at the peak of her work stress.

70 E Robinson et al, 'Eating attentively: a systematic review and meta-analysis of the effect of food intake memory and awareness on eating', *The American Journal of Clinical Nutrition*, 97:4 (2013), https://doi.org/10.3945/ajcn.112.045245

71 G Pizzino et al, 'Oxidative stress: Harms and benefits for human health', *Oxidative Medicine and Cellular Longevity* (27 July 2017), www.ncbi.nlm.nih.gov/pmc/articles/PMC5551541, accessed 1 April 2023

72 J Freese et al, 'The sedentary (r)evolution: Have we lost our metabolic flexibility?' *F1000Research*, 6:1787 (2018), https://doi.org/10.12688/f1000research.12724.2

73 C Vette, 'Can intermittent fasting improve your gut health?' *Zoe* (7 November 2022), https://joinzoe.com/learn/intermittent-fasting-gut-health, accessed 13 February 2023

74 Water Science School, 'The water in you: Water and the human body', USGS (22 May 2019), www.usgs.gov/special-topics/water-science-school/science/water-you-water-and-human-body, accessed 9 March 2023

75 MCT oil is a supplement made from a type of fat called medium-chain triglycerides. MCT molecules are smaller than those in most of the fats you eat, which makes them easier to digest.

76 You might recall from Chapter Four that autophagy is the body's natural process of self-cleaning, when it gets rid of damaged proteins and other dysfunctional cells.

77 JA Levine, 'Non-exercise activity thermogenesis (NEAT)', *Best Practice and Research Clinical Endocrinology and Metabolism*, 16:4 (2002), https://doi.org/10.1053/beem.2002.0227

78 A Whittaker et al, 'Daily stair climbing is associated with decreased risk for the metabolic syndrome', *BMC Public Health* (2021), https://doi.org/10.1186/s12889-021-10965-9

79 K Nunez, 'What are the advantages of nose breathing vs. mouth breathing?' *Healthline* (1 February 2021), www.healthline.com/health/nose-breathing, accessed 13 February 2023

80 S Vadlamani, 'What is forest bathing? Discover 6 key health benefits', *Happiness.com* (no date), www.happiness.com/magazine/health-body/benefits-of-forest-bathing, accessed 13 February 2023

81 AJ Crum and EJ Langer, 'Mindset Matters: Exercise and the placebo effect', *Psychological Science* (February 2007), https://doi.org/10.1111/j.1467-9280.2007.01867.x

82 J Hoffman, 'Resistance training and injury prevention', American College of Sports Medicine (2017), https://www.acsm.org/docs/default-source/files-for-resource-library/smb-resistance-training-and-injury-prevention.pdf, accessed 13 February 2023

83 JB Kreher and JB Schwartz, 'Overtraining syndrome: A practical guide', *Sports Health*, 4:2 (2012), pp128–138, https://doi.org/10.1177/1941738111434406

84 Mentioned earlier in the book, Wim Hoff (aka 'the Iceman') popularised and championed the benefits of cold plunging.

85 E Suni, 'How much sleep do we really need?', Sleep Foundation (updated 29 August 2022), www.sleepfoundation.org/how-sleep-works/how-much-sleep-do-we-really-need, accessed 13 February 2023

86 C Blume et al, 'Effects of light on human circadian rhythms, sleep and mood', *Somnologie*, 23 (2019), https://doi.org/10.1007/s11818-019-00215-x

87 For example: LA Ostrin, 'Ocular and systemic melatonin and the influence of light exposure', *Clin Exp Optom*, 102(2) (2019), pp99–108, https://doi.org/10.1111/cxo.12824

88 J Chaput et al, 'Sleep timing, sleep consistency, and health in adults: A systematic review', *Applied Physiology, Nutrition, and Metabolism*, 45:10 (suppl 2) (2020), https://doi.org/10.1139/apnm-2020-0032

89 CE Kline, 'The bidirectional relationship between exercise and sleep: Implications for exercise adherence and sleep improvement', *American Journal of Lifestyle Medicine*, 8:6 (2014), https://doi.org/10.1177/1559827614544437

90 D Jakubowicz et al, 'High caloric intake at breakfast vs. dinner differentially influences weight loss of overweight and obese women', *Obesity* (Silver Spring) (December 2013), https://doi.org/10.1002/oby.20460

91 IM Colrain et al, 'Chapter 24: Alcohol and the sleeping brain', *Handbook of Clinical Neurology* (2014), https://doi.org/10.1016/B978-0-444-62619-6.00024-0

92 Some people are better able to metabolise caffeine, so it may have a lesser impact on their sleep. However, why take the risk of any disruption to your sleep from drinking coffee late in the evening?

93 MP Walker and R Stickgold, 'Sleep-dependent learning and memory consolidation', *Neuron*, 44:1 (2004), https://doi.org/10.1016/j.neuron.2004.08.031

94 V Drago et al, 'The correlation between sleep and creativity', *Nature Precedings* (2010), https://doi.org/10.1038/npre.2010.4266.1

95 E Van der Helm et al, 'REM sleep depotentiates amygdala activity to previous emotional experiences', *Current Biology*, 21 (2011), https://doi.org/10.1016/j.cub.2011.10.052

96 Deep vein thrombosis (DVT) is a medical condition that occurs when a blood clot forms in a deep vein. There are several factors that can contribute to this potentially fatal condition and high-altitude travel for prolonged periods has been shown to be a significant factor. See: N Gupta and MZ Ashraf, 'Exposure to high altitude: A risk factor for venous thromboembolism?', *Seminars in Thrombosis and Hemostasis* (March 2012), https://doi.org/10.1055/s-0032-1301413

97 M Tamaki et al, 'Night watch in one brain hemisphere during sleep associated with the first-night effect in humans', *Current Biology*, 26:9 (2016), pp1190–1194, https://doi.org/10.1016/j.cub.2016.02.063

98 A popular acronym meaning 'fear of missing out'.

99 No author, 'Deaths from older adult falls', CDC (no date), www.cdc.gov/falls/data/fall-deaths.html, accessed 13 February 2023

100 As we are writing this book, Jim is training for the CrossFit Open where he will compete with athletes from all over the world, some of whom have been training their whole lives.

Further Reading

Here are some books that we have found interesting and informative on our own wellness journeys. Some of them are quoted throughout the book. Enjoy!

Mindset

Bailey C, *Hyper Focus: How to work less and achieve more* (Pan Macmillan, 2019)

Brown RP and Gerbarg PM, *The Healing Power of Breath: Simple techniques to reduce stress and anxiety, enhance concentration, and balance your emotions* (Shambhala, 2012)

Burnett D, *The Idiot Brain: A neuroscientist explains what your head is really up to* (Guardian Faber, 2016)

Chaskalson M, *Mindfulness in Eight Weeks: The revolutionary eight-week plan to clear your mind and calm your life* (HarperCollins, 2014)

Chaskalson M, *The Mindful Workplace: Developing resilient individuals and resonant organizations with MBSR* (Wiley-Blackwell, 2011)

Clear J, *Atomic Habits: An easy and proven way to build good habits and break old ones* (Penguin Books, 2018)

Duhigg C, *The Power of Habit: Why we do what we do in life and in business* (Random House, 2012)

Everett G, *Tough: Building true mental, physical and emotional toughness for success and fulfilment* (Catalyst Athletics, 2021)

Hoff W, *The Wim Hoff Method: Activate your potential, transcend your limits* (Penguin Books, 2020)

Rao SS, *Happiness at Work: Be resilient, motivated, and successful – no matter what* (McGraw Hill, 2010)

Sinek S, *Start With Why: How great leaders inspire everyone to take action* (Penguin Business, 2009)

Tolle E, *The Power of Now: A guide to spiritual enlightenment* (Namaste Publishing, 2004)

Nutrition

Bryan L, *Healthy Meal Prep: 100+ make-ahead recipes and quick-assembly meals,* (Clarkson Potter Publishers, 2022)

Hyman M, *Eat Fat Get Thin: Why the fat we eat is the key to sustained weight loss and vibrant health* (Hodder & Stoughton, 2016)

Hyman M, *The Pegan Diet: 21 practical principles for reclaiming your health in a nutritionally confusing world* (Yellow Kite, 2021)

Li W, *Eat to Beat Disease: The body's five defence systems and the foods that could save your life* (Penguin Random House, 2019)

Pelz M, *Fast Like a Girl: A woman's guide to using the healing power of fasting to burn fat, boost energy, and balance hormones* (Hay House, 2022)

Pontzer H, *Slow Burn: The misunderstood science of metabolism* (Penguin Random House, 2021)

Shanahan C and Shanahan L, *Deep Nutrition: Why your genes need traditional food* (Flatiron Books, second edition, 2016)

Sonnenburg J and Sonnenburg E, *The Good Gut: Taking control of your weight, your mood, and your long-term health* (Penguin Books, 2016)

Movement

Kilham CS, *The Five Tibetans: Five dynamic exercises for health, energy, and personal power* (Healing Arts Press, new edition, 2011)

Mittleman S and Callan K, *Slow Burn: Burn fat faster by exercising slower* (Harper, 2000)

Phillips S, *Strength for Life: Shape your body, sharpen your mind, energize your life* (Ballantine Books, 2008)

Starrett K and Cordoza G, *Becoming a Supple Leopard: The ultimate guide to resolving pain, preventing injury, and optimizing athletic performance* (Victory Belt Publishing, second edition, 2015)

Sleep

Walker M, *Why We Sleep: The new science of sleep and dreams* (Penguin Books, 2018)

Panda S, *The Circadian Code: Lose weight, supercharge your energy and transform your health from morning to midnight* (Vermilion, 2018)

Other

Ashton J, *The Self-Care Solution: A year of becoming happier, healthier and fitter – one month at a time* (JLA Enterprises Corporation, 2019)

Hyman M, *Young Forever: The secrets to living your longest, healthiest life* (Yellow Kite, 2023)

Know L, *Mitochondria and the Future of Medicine: The key to understanding disease, chronic illness, aging and life itself* (Chelsea Green Publishing, 2018)

Sisson M, *The Primal Blueprint: Reprogramme your genes for effortless weight loss, vibrant health, and boundless energy* (Primal Blueprint Publishing, fourth edition, 2019)

Acknowledgements

Writing this book has been an amazing experience for both of us. It helped us to crystallise our experience of rediscovering our health, and to flesh out the TAKEOFF model, which we hope will inspire you to start your own lifelong wellness journey.

We are grateful to the amazing friends and family who joined us for our very first pilot programmes. Your results were encouraging and your feedback was invaluable. Our conversations inspired us to dig even further into the science, develop a solid framework and put this book together. Eszter, Petra, Jan, Dani, Judit, Mari, Olgi, Kieran, Natalie, thank you for your support and willingness to come with us on this journey.

Many thanks also to our beta readers: Emese, Henning, Deirdre, Armin, Marco, Simon and Declan. Your views and insights helped this to be an even more powerful message.

Melinda, what would we do without you? Thank you for coming on our test runs, beta reading this book, cheering us on and just being a constant ray of sunshine. Your insights and energy added so much to this book.

Thank you to the super professional Rethink team: Anke, Kathy and Lisa for the incredible work you did on the manuscript to turn it into this book. In particular, we would like to thank our wonderful writing coach, Alison, without whom, the process would have been a lot more challenging and not as much fun. You were an inspiration.

Thank you!

The Authors

Natasa is a co-founder of Wizz Air and has spent her corporate career in communications and general management roles. At the peak of her career, she set up and managed Wizz Air Ukraine. She holds a Master's Degree in Positive Leadership and Strategy. Her passion lies in nutrition, female hormonal health and breathwork. She is a certified nutrition and ICF accredited Gestalt coach.

Jim is a corporate lawyer. As a general counsel, he spent most of his career keeping large companies such as Ryanair, Etihad and Uber out of trouble. Jim is an avid CrossFitter and a qualified Level 1 CrossFit coach. He also has a certificate in exercise physiology from Stanford University Center for Health Education. His passions are human evolution and creating working environments that promote (non-exercise) functional movement.

⊕ https://wellnesstory.world

in Natasa: www.linkedin.com/in/natasa-kazmer

in Jim: www.linkedin.com/in/jim-callaghan-wellnesstory